Lebanon at the Brink

A condensed analysis of the causes and proposed solutions centered on Dollarization

Dr. Sarkis Joseph Khoury

Preface

The problems of Lebanon are so severe as to require dramatic changes to protect the welfare of millions of people that have grown dependent on a government that is no longer able to protect their wellbeing, nor promise a brighter future. Lebanon has been limping from one bad economic/political strategy to another for far too long.

This book looks at the causes of the current crisis, and identifies those key factors that have become deep and systematic, and allowed a self-selected minority of traditionalists to create new privileges ever at the expense of the average citizen. The net results are a country that is one of the most indebted in the world unable to pay its creditors, more people living in poverty, a collapsing currency affecting mostly those with small savings, a flailing democracy, and an infrastructure that is in desperate need of repair and expansion.

The Lebanese people have had it with Corruption and with a currency that is barely accepted even within Lebanon. A move to the dollar as the currency of choice (medium of exchange) as a store of value and as a unit of account has started long ago. No Lebanese today prefer holding the Lira instead of the dollar. It is time to use the dollar exclusively as the currency of Lebanon-that is abandoning the Lira altogether. This will bring economic stability, a large flow of foreign investment, and allow the BDL to focus on the stability, efficiency, compliance with international banking standards, and liquidity of the banking system in Lebanon instead of spending its time and resources to defend an indefensible PEG.

"We recommend Dollarization."

Acknowledgments

This book was prepared to analyze the economic crisis in Lebanon and its underlying causes and to propose a workable solution that will stabilize the economy and reduce the disruptions in the lives and welfare of the people of Lebanon. The book was not commissioned by any organization, nor is it written on behalf of any political or economic group in Lebanon. Dr. Khoury has studied International Finance at Wharton and has been studying financial structures and currency regimes for decades. He felt that it is time to put them to use to help Lebanon.

The book is simply the result of intellectual curiosity and my well-earned expertise. Dr. Khoury has been committed to the progress and the stability of Lebanon, the country of his birth since he left Lebanon 50 years ago...

Numerous scholars and political observers have been kind enough to discuss key issues with the authors. None of them is responsible for any opinion or discussion in the book. Our thanks go to Dr. Clas Wihlborg, Dr. Stephen Hanke, Dr. Poorna Pal, and Dr. Charles Chartouni, and others. Dr. Khoury relied on numerous articles in Google and in Google Scholar as sources of information and perspective.

All the chapters in the book, except Chapter 4, were fully written by Dr. Khoury. Chapter 4 was largely conceived by Dr. Khoury. Dr. Poorna Pal produced all the graphs and tables in this chapter and some of the content. He owns 7 percent of the net proceeds of the book. Substantial input by Dr. Mahmoud Arayssi is acknowledged with gratitude

All comments on any part of the book will be welcome.

Dedication

I dedicate this book to the memory of my father: Joseph Sarkis Khoury, who never finished primary school, and never fully understood what I was doing in America and why I was writing books and articles. He never left Lebanon.

When asked why he always answered "Lashou."

Table of Contents

Chapter 1
The Eight Fundamental Disequilibria: Undermining the Long Term Stability of Lebanon and the Commitment of its Diaspora

Introduction

There is in Lebanon today a semblance of calm, beauty, modernity, elegance, charm, incredible nightlife, great culture, delicious food of all sorts, an overwhelming history, cars, more cars, and then even more cars. All was disrupted by a new invader: The Corona Virus.

The political patchwork that is Lebanon appears to be under control, and the risks of civil war or conflict with Lebanon's neighbors are minimal at this time. But beneath all of it, there is a political structure that lacks great leadership and stability. Listening to some Lebanese politicians, one may conclude that all is well in paradise. Others think that the country is going to hell in a basket.

The Lebanon Spring had started in 2005 with feverish enthusiasm and conviction that building a new Lebanon is possible and timely. Massive demonstrations began immediately after the assassination of Prime Minister Hariri on February 14, 2005. On the 18th, the BLUE (the symbol of the revolution) covered the entire center of Beirut. It was about Freedom, Accountability, Sovereignty, and Independence. Astonishingly, there were also massive demonstrations in opposition to the departure of Syrians, who had ruled in Lebanon for almost thirty years.

The CEDAR Revolution backed strongly by the Bush Administration, found solace and vindication in the departure of the Syrians from Lebanon on April 27, 2005.

The Syrians who had left Lebanon from the front door came

back from the backdoor with their allies, the Iranians, who support and finance Hizbollah. All the established figures of Lebanon's political system stayed on the scene and became further entrenched. Berri, the Speaker of the Parliament in Lebanon today, stated at the time, "The Cedar Revolution took Lebanon 60 years back."

Lebanon, much like the rest of the Arab world, is suffering from a large set of issues that caused the revolution to fizzle. The activists thought their revolution was about principles, but it turned out to be more about their personalities. They thought it was about a new democratic structure, it turned out to be about the segmentation of Lebanon into political fiefdoms that are not democratic. They thought it was about creating an independent Lebanon as a master of its destiny. Still, foreign interventions multiplied became more intense and did not allow Lebanon to achieve their desired independence. Some Lebanese were even yearning for the French Mandate, incredibly.

The meritocratic standards, once considered achievable in Lebanon, were skewed by raw power politics and the lack of overlapping consensus insofar as the legitimacy of the Nation-State and its most suitable type of governance. Power politics, exercised by some political groups, have warped the mechanics of governance and relegated professional issues of governance to the backburner.

A new 'revolution" was attempted in the year 2019 with a new foci: Corruption, decent governance, and economic malaise. It was a flash with surface results.

The above results could have been easily anticipated, as Lebanon suffers from EIGHT Fundamental Disequilibria that continue to ravage its political structure as well as depress its possibilities. Should the political class decide not to address them, they could lead to increased balkanization of the Lebanese society, along with civil unrest, subversive activities, and massive migration. The latter being the most likely one. We review the various disequilibria with the first being a structured one, again through foreign influence.

1- Post-Colonial Political Arrangement

From the moment of its inception back in 1943, Lebanon was structured to be different based on its religious distributions in by affiliation and cooperation with the French.

An agreement was forged where the President, a Maronite Christian, the Prime Minister a Sunni Muslim, and the Speaker of the Parliament, a member of the Shiite faith. Nothing was said about the talent distribution in Lebanon, the level of education within each group, and the ultimate emergence of a meritocracy.

Each religious group began to act with a sense of entitlement to certain positions and a certain level of political power. As the population grew within each religious grouping, the power center shifted, out-migration levels shifted, and education levels shifted. The old understandings and the political equation began to fray. Adding to the internal pressures was the rise of Iran and Saudi Arabia as potent regional players, the competition between Sunni Islam and

Shia Islam, and the ineffectual presidents of Lebanon after President's Chehab and Chamoun. The perceived political equilibrium descended into internal competition for power at the expense of the national good and national stability.

2- The Taef Agreement of 1989

At its core, this Agreement was supposed to provide an equilibrium between the religions in terms of access to political power and make Lebanon more governable. Instead, it created a poorly governed country: A Christian President who was restricted in most of his powers; a Prime Minister who typically spends his term as a caretaker, spending money he does not have and making certain frequent trips to Saudi Arabia for political and economic cover; and a Speaker of the Parliament who can, singlehandedly, suspend whatever exists of the democratic process in Lebanon, while massive accusations of corruption swirl around him.

The 50-50 division of power between Christians and Muslims deepened the confessionalism in Lebanon and created a weaker state. It was supposed to be applied to the top government posts. It became the norm for all appointments across all the grades classified by the central government. It returned Lebanon to the days of zaameh and clientelism, where a political leader hands out positions in the government in exchange for loyalty and votes. The net results are a massive misallocation of resources: posts going to incompetent actors, massive abuse of budgetary allocations producing, for example, "one teacher for every four students" in some schools in the South, and massive, unexplained hiring's in many sectors or institutions that have nothing to do with institutional needs and efficiency requirements. Employment at the Central Bank of Lebanon (BDL) almost tripled in about 20 years, etc. The World Bank commented on the economic effects of such sectarian policies in a 2015 report:

"The need to maintain a sectarian "balance of power" within institutions, reflected in both staffing and a division of responsibilities in resource allocation, resulting in sectarian interests being prioritized over the need for equitable and adequate provision of services, and a general lack of transparency and accountability."

All the political and sectarian accommodations translated into huge budget deficits, massive borrowing, and general economic instability that will be the focus on the remaining chapters.

They also led to a more profound political disequilibrium. The only strategy that worked was deployed by Hizbollah: Split the Christians, keep the Druze at bay, and you shall control the politics of Lebanon. Add to this a massive security apparatus, and the number of Shia members in the Parliament mattered little except for possible parliamentary maneuvers.

The Troika supposed to govern Lebanon and provide it with balance, and more representative democracy led to weak governance.

Democracy presupposes a voice for the majority. The majority in Lebanon is Muslim. But the political majority does not need to be Muslim. The 50-50 proposition could, therefore, be used simply to secure particular government positions that have been historically handed out on religious bases. The religious majority yielded to a political majority in Lebanon made up of Christians and Muslims working on ideological and self-interested grounds.

This majority takes direction from outside Lebanon, mostly through Hizbollah, who found allies in President Aoun and his political party. A new state of disequilibrium was produced because of population distributions, political alignments, and brute force being used to threaten and often to liquidate political enemies.

The political minority in the government can simply threaten the majority and try to create stalemates, ultimately bringing down a government. They call themselves the LOYAL OPPOSITION. They fizzled but continued shouting from the sidelines.

The ruling coalition is bringing neither reform nor hope, nor change. They conveniently forgot all the objectives of the Cedar Revolution.

3- **The considerable disequilibrium between the government, and the shadow (Mezzanine) government**

It was 1982; the Shia population in Lebanon was the bottom of the educational, economic, health care, and political scales in Lebanon. Poverty was everywhere, and too many young men measured streets. They accounted for one-third of the

Lebanese population. A change had to come.
Their religious leader at the time was Sayyed Musa Al Sadr, a cleric with an imposing personality, significant convictions, and commitment to the plurality of Lebanon. He had been trained in Iran. Their socio-political organization was Amal run by Nabih Berri (currently the Speaker of the Parliament). Amal was perceived at the time as a check on the PLO movements in Southern Lebanon and enjoyed considerable support from Damascus, which was run by fellow co-religionists.
The Israeli invasion of Lebanon in 1982 created an occupation force in Lebanon, especially in the South and in Beirut; Israel controlled about ten percent of its territory, and it lasted eighteen years. Israel invaded on June 6, 1982, to stem the attacks and the rising power of the PLO. Amal was not able to control the PLO actions. Amal's focus became more political, especially after the death of his spiritual Leader Imam Sadr.
Iran saw a great opportunity in Lebanon to create a client organization by uniting the disparate Shia groups that are opposed to the PLO actions in the South and that are virulently anti-Israel. They worked with Mohammad Fadlallah, Imad Mughnieh, and Ragheb Harb. The first Secretary of the new group was Abbas Al Mussawi, who was later assassinated by Israel. A Shia cleric by the name of Hasan Nasrallah, opposed to America's power in the region and its strong support of Israel, emerged as the leader of the new group: The Party of God (Hizbollah). Iran was a strong

financial supporter of the group. Hizbollah set up substantial infrastructures for the Shia in the South of Lebanon and recruited a massive number of its youth after the Israeli invasion. They managed to control the Palestinian camps, and they quickly became belligerent as well as a political force to reckon with. After the Israeli departure from Southern Lebanon, they solidified their control over the South of Lebanon and started an Islamic Revolution mirroring that of Iran.

The political atmospherics in Lebanon were conveniently accommodating to their expansion. The competing notions and sources of legitimacy represented by the Nation-State and the transnational ideologies of the Arab and Islamic "Ummah (transnational community)" were expressed through foreign interventions and curtailed sovereignty. The state of endemic instability has favored shameless opportunism and predatory behavior, which distorted the very notion of the common good and skewed the process of governance. The financial and economic pitfalls of governance, as well as their overall incidence of practical politics and daily governance, reflect the discrepancies between the mandates of a democratic government and the undermined sovereignty of a country made hostage to an embedded crisis of legitimacy. Unable to contain the disruptive dynamics of intertwined domestic and regional power politics, Lebanon was relegated towards a state of structural instability.

Hizbollah didn't only challenge the Shia community but

sought and achieved what some had considered impossible: strong influence over the Lebanese political process and its electoral results despite massive U.S. objections and countermeasures. They entered the Lebanese Parliament in 1992 by winning 12 seats out of 128. In 2005 they won 14 seats. In 2018 they won 13 seats. They allied with Amal, and now they have 29 seats. They have further created an alliance with the Free Patriotic Movement that had later endorsed the Presidency of Michel Aoun (the current President). They had also managed to control 21% of all municipalities in Lebanon and have three ministers in the Administration.

If this were not enough, they relied on the support they were receiving from Syria, and especially Iran. On their military presence and their infiltration of the various military and security forces in Lebanon to achieve at least a political stalemate when they are opposed to a policy or a particular government appointment.

Now Hizbollah largely determines:

- When Lebanon goes to war- They showed it in 2006;
- The basics of Lebanon's foreign policy;
- Who governs, and who is to be politically neutralized;
- The distribution of the national wealth;
- Who represents the Christians in Shia populated areas;
- Which government post is reserved for its allies; and
- Who receives and entertains Iranian officials in Lebanon, and the requisite coordination,

implementation and mentoring by Iran.
Their influence extends well beyond Lebanon. They were quite active and even decisive in the Battle against ISIL. They played a significant role in Iraq and Yemen. And, their presence in various parts of the Arab World, Africa and especially Latin America is substantial and compelling. They successfully recruited, if not co-opted, the immigrant Shia communities in various parts of the world.
One must admire, parenthetically, their successful political maneuvers, no matter its nature, and consequence. Even Ehud Barak acknowledged that Israel's presence in Lebanon had created Hizbollah.
Saudi Arabia and its allies in Lebanon sought to stem the tide of Iranian influence in Lebanon to shape the politics of Lebanon. The effects of their massive investments in Lebanon, as well as their considerable financial support of various political groups, including fundamentalists, have not always been successful, yet they continue to try.
Hizbollah, characterized by the United States as a "terrorist group," is today the center of resistance against Israeli policies, tactics, and military moves, including works with Arab governments to enhance its effectiveness, despite the announced neutrality policy of Lebanon.

4- The Disequilibrium Produced by Local vs. Foreign allegiances

The following historical realities must be observed:
The Lebanese are always looking outside of Lebanon for

political backing and legitimization. Internal popular support is often vitiated by foreign dictates.

Syria had ruled Lebanon for almost three decades with an iron fist, abused its women, stole its coffers, and terrorized its leaders, and often murdered them, all in the name of security.

The Iranians, in need of a client state bordering Israel and the Mediterranean, have achieved the unachievable – complete control over the security of vast areas in Lebanon.

The Americans and the Europeans continue to interfere (influence) in Lebanon's politics but are now finding the Russians at the doorsteps of Lebanon and their influence decline.

The net effects of Russian and Iranian influence and ideologies in the region and in Lebanon can be transformative if they take hold (e.g., central planning, weak legal structures, lack of democratic accountability, etc.) They will change regional realignment, the economic policies to deal with the current crisis, and Lebanon's national stability and competitiveness in the world economy.

Shockingly, two failed states in terms of economic performance: Russia and Iran have co-opted with the West in terms of political influence in Lebanon. Neither can help Lebanon in addressing the current economic crisis. They are content to refer the problems to the World Bank or the IMF, especially when their hands are full in Syria and their domestic economies.

5- The Huge Income Disequilibrium

According to the World Inequality Database, the bottom 50% of the Lebanese population earns 10.5% of the national income. The wealthiest 1% "earns about 25% of GDP, close to the highest share in the Middle East, itself one of the most unequal regions in the world."

The poor continue to struggle in Lebanon. Should the current crisis continue, half the Lebanese population will be living in poverty? The rich continue to ignore the concept of fair wages, excellent benefits, and the right working conditions. The economy prospers as it works for the comfort of the few and of foreigners. It is almost always the case that the fruits of business go to the owners of the business, with little for the workers and managers that make it all work.

The recent massive protests in Lebanon in 2019/ 2020 were triggered by the $6 tax on Whatsapp announced by the government in order to collect $250 million annually. The protesters have had enough of abusive governance. The National Army that is supposed to defend the country against foreign intrusions was in the streets beating up and threatening demonstrators.

And the Oligarchs remained unrepentant!

This will get even worse once the gas has been extracted from the ground, and the proceeds are divided between the corrupt elite. The dividends of Lebanon's energy reserves will not reach the poor Lebanese.

The group that was in charge of splitting the spoils from

Lebanon's oil and gas showed the world a master plan for what robbing the state looks like. We will discuss the scheme in a chapter to follow.
The rich are walking the streets with their half-yard cigar and the poor with their shoeshine boxes.

6-The Disequilibrium in Ethics

Lebanon is, lamentably, a corrupt country!

According to Trading Economics and Transparency.Org, Lebanon ranks 137 among 180 countries in terms of Corruption. It is on par with Kenya, Liberia, and Papua New Guinea. Ranking ahead of Lebanon are Togo, Mali, and Mexico.

Performance, transparency, and accountability remain alien to Lebanon
Every government employee has expertly manufactured a license to impose his/her tax (corruption level) on every transaction. Corruption files are open and then closed. No one goes to jail for Corruption. This encourages Corruption. At a lecture the author (SJK) gave in Lebanon, he asked a large number of students in a Christian university if they would cheat if they thought they could get away with it. Every hand went up. This is what the young generation is learning from their leaders.
Even the court system is a bidding process. The highest

bidder typically prevails.

This substantially explains the massive immigration numbers by recent college graduates. Almost all the graduates of one university in Lebanon in the field of nursing and pharmacy leave Lebanon upon graduation. Engineers and medical graduates are often in tow.

7- **Disequilibrium in Opportunities**

Lebanon may well be the biggest exporter of brainpower per capita, with most of the recent emigration being Christian.

Those who receive college degrees are doomed to get work below their real value or risk participating in an abusive work environment. Their escape valve is immigration so they may harness their brainpower and their training consistent with the many technological developments in the world and the trends in compensation,

Numerous foreign companies, many from the U.S., tried to set up research or production centers in Lebanon. Many of the projects were reduced or eliminated. The typical complaints are about Corruption and excessive regulation.

8- **Disequilibrium in access to Justice**

Legal cases that could be easily resolved in days languish for years in Lebanese courts. Open bidding about the bribe in a case takes place in the court itself. People sell properties to get access to qualified, well connected legal counselors. Fighting the oligarchs in the court system is known to be impossible, yet many try.

Ministers of Justice are appointed based on political affiliation and how they advantage the political party that

promoted their hiring.
The injustices permeate the system in insurance cases as well as accident cases, murder cases, divorce cases (it is scandalous what happens to women rights in cases of divorce across all religious groups), inheritance cases, nationalization cases, access to schools, loans in the banking system, and the list goes on.
Even the right to vote is diluted. Elections are postponed or canceled. Competing candidates are threatened or bribed into withdrawal. And elections could only be done by voting for a "list," as was done in the last election. Choosing a single candidate from the list, typically headed by an oligarch, was not allowed.
Clear and common believed cases involving public or business corruption get their files opened, but only for the appearance of Justice.
Illustrious cases like that of Bank Al Madina, a clear example of money laundering (more on this in later chapters), forgery of documents, and high political patronage, are opened and then soon closed when the real story is about to be told. A fallen person, Rana Qoleilat, in this case, was demonized and jailed in quarters that resemble a first-class hotel. The money simply vanished, and all the perpetrators kept their loot.

Conclusion

The disequilibria we discussed in this chapter are real and serious. They must be addressed if Lebanon is to chart a new path towards a bright future.

The lessons from Lebanon are harsh, indeed. The Lebanese government is intent on strengthening the relationship between the Lebanese immigrant communities all over the world and Lebanon. It must recognize, however, that it is one thing to long for one's roots. Still, another is to ignore the risk profile of Lebanon, which is getting worse compared to other very lucrative international opportunities.

The Lebanese government will be well served to set up certain panels of experts (technocrats) drawn from all around the world with considerable executive powers:

- To manage Lebanon's energy resources.
- To improve its educational system.
- To reduce pollution of all forms.
- To develop strategies and processes to stop the brain drain from Lebanon.
- To improve the democratic processes and secure fair, honest elections.
- To have competent workers protection with appropriate health care and retirement benefits.
- To make Lebanon hospitable for foreign investment by improving its infrastructure and eliminating Corruption.

These measures will reduce the national risk profile of

Lebanon and improve the flow of investment dollars in the country.

The Lebanese Diaspora can partner with the Lebanese political and economic structures/personalities to demonstrate its love and commitment towards Lebanon. Their level of expertise in all the mentioned domains is beyond reproach, and their experiences are enormous.

Western and Latin American countries, as well as all Arab countries that have benefited tremendously from the skills and the entrepreneurship of Lebanese immigrants, must support this transformational effort. The United States must also lead. This will help create a veritable oasis of stability in the Middle East based on open markets, free-market principles, coexistence among both religious and ethnic groups, and negotiated agreements instead of wars-all within a truly democratic structure.

America will benefit enormously if it commits to reform in Lebanon by demonstrating that it is dedicated to constructive engagement in smaller countries like Lebanon. Also, by proving to the world that a new multicultural, multi-religious, and multi ideological Lebanon functioning in harmony and prosperity is indeed a model for the world to emulate.

Chapter 2
The Emasculation of the Central Lebanese State and Corruption

Introduction

This chapter seeks to establish connections between political events and the economic stability of Lebanon. We consider specific episodes in the history of Lebanon since the 1970s and forward. We chose them to emphasize the drift, often radical, in Lebanese policies, the destructive laissez-faire attitude toward political oligarchs and their deeds, and the shifting political ideologies, as well as their currency within the Lebanese body politic, are detrimental to the national good. The traditional view and expectation that the Lebanese Diaspora will for a fact come to the rescue no matter the developments within Lebanon (political, economic, religious, social, etc.) is at best naïve because of its assumption that foreign investors are not at all concerned with risks/ return tradeoffs of investment opportunities in Lebanon. The sentimental view of Lebanon is disappearing, the resident Lebanese must understand.

Lebanon is very tribal. The members of the tribe need to feel the merits and influence of their leader. This is explored through employment opportunities, bringing government money to bear on certain local projects, securing someone's release from prison, talking to a judge about leniency, demonstrated role on the national scene, and even in accepting gifts from their harvest. But all leaders are not quite the same, and the national pie has a finite size. Therefore, prominent leaders like Frangieh, Hariri, Gemayel, jumblat, and the others had to compete for the

bigger share of the pie. Each of them, consequently, acted as worthy of being a President someday regardless of effort, education, plans for the country, criminal background, or even the region they came from.
The tribal influence and the appeasement of its members do not always translate into national growth and stability. Zgharta had done well when Franjieh became President, but how well did Lebanon do? Did that presidency produce a transition into a more centralized authority for the state, a more efficient government, more reconciliation among the various political parties, better infrastructure for the country, better schools, less immigration and better jobs for the youth, a more peaceful and less corrupt country, etc.? In many cases the answer was no. Few Presidents of Lebanon proved that they were, in fact, worthy of the position and able to solidify the interests and the authority of the state in the pursuit of the public good.
The emasculation of the state and its rampant Corruption can explain to a great extent the problems existing in Lebanon today, the increased tension with its neighbors, and the decreased significance of Lebanon on the international stage.

A Few Historic Notes

The Cairo Agreement of 1969 had marked the first egregious case of the Lebanese government ceding sovereignty and associated authority over a large portion of Lebanon to the

Palestinian Armed Struggle Command. The Agreement was negotiated in Cairo while the presence of the Egyptians Ministers of War and of Foreign Affairs representing President Gamal Abdelnasser of Egypt (the defender of his revolution and the rights of the Palestinians to have a homeland) with considerable input from Saudi Arabia eager to support fellow Sunnis. They were dispossessed by Israel and pushed out of Jordan. General Emile Boustany, the leader of the Lebanese Army, drunk on the possibility of becoming the next President of Lebanon, leading the Lebanese delegation. Yasser Arafat represented the Palestinians. The text of the Agreement was never yet published. In exchange for less interference with the affairs of the city of Beirut, General Boustany signed the Agreement on April 20, 1970. It removed the 300,000 Palestinians under UNRWA support from the supervision of the Lebanese Army as well as the Lebanese intelligence services. Lebanon became a base for the Palestinian guerilla movement. The Agreement:

"Established the right of the Palestinians in Lebanon to join the Palestinian revolution to 'join the Palestinian revolution through armed struggle.' Also, it allowed the Palestinians to legally control their refugee camps in Lebanon and also to launch attacks against Israel from South Lebanon".

A State within a State was born. No one could have predicted the tragic outcomes, the political and military conflicts, the massacres, and the political treachery that followed it. Palestinians supported by the Lebanese

National Movement, a Sunni group in Beirut, were visible in their freedom of movement and abuses within Beirut. A Lebanese citizen traveling to the South of Lebanon needed special permission. The author received it to travel to the city of Tyre in the South of Lebanon.

The irritations of Israel were obvious. Internecine warfare was observed continuously. Fadi Frem and Fouad Abou Nader succeeded Bachir as chiefs of staff of the Lebanese Forces. The Palestinian conduct in the South was also irritating the Lebanese Shia population. Lebanon paid the price all along.

The ire of the Christian population in the South and the city of Beirut was serious and rising. The Lebanese Army was unable to contain the actions of the Palestinians. In April 1975, a civil war broke out with massive casualties and destruction on both sides. Numerous Christian and Muslim families then left Lebanon, and the country sunk in the process into a state of the absurd. President Frangieh asked Syria to intervene, and they did so, allegedly, to protect the Maronite population.

In the South, the situation became even worse as Israel invaded Lebanon in March 1978. The conflict further escalated, and Israel invaded, occupied Southern Lebanon in 1982, and expelled the PLO from southern Lebanon.

President Amine Gemayel canceled the Cairo Agreement in June 1987.

Meanwhile, the fracturing of Lebanon at all levels continued. Israel managed to get Bachir Gemayel elected

President. He was killed in 1982 before he took office, and the speculation continues until now as to who did it.
New actors appeared on the scene with a considerable amount of military power and willingness to use it with no reference to any government authority, and often in a direct challenge to it. Among the Christians, the parties with effectiveness and authority in various parts of Lebanon were: The Phalange, the Ahrar, the Marada, The Lebanese Forces, and The South Lebanon Army. After Bachir's death, Fouad Abi Naader became the head of The Lebanese Forces only to be removed by a coup orchestrated by Geagea and Hobeika.
In March 1985. Geagea was able to remove Hobeika, who fled to Syria and later settled in Zahle.
The 1990 Geagea disbanded The Lebanese Forces sold most of its arms and ceded what was left to the Lebanese Army after a deadly fight with General Aoun and the Syrians. All Christian militias then became political actors.
Only two nongovernment military forces, well-armed and willing to protect their interests even by the power of arms or by threats, remained on the scene: The Armed Palestinian forces and Hizbollah.
The latter increased in numbers since, in potency (military and political), and in their own ability to twist political arms to affect its desirable vision for Lebanon while protecting the interests of the Shia community in Lebanon. It can be argued that they constitute "a State within a State."
The departure of the Syrian forces from Lebanon in 2005,

driven out by the Cedar revolution and various U.S. Congressional Resolutions and threats by President George W. Bush, further consolidated the power of Hizbollah-an unintended consequence. It manifested its independent streak in the war with Israel in 2006 that ended up destroying a lot of areas in Lebanon by vicious Israeli bombardment. The conflict ended with both parties accepting U.N. Resolution 1701. Before that, they were accused of the murder of Prime Minister Shafiq Hariri back in February 2005. (The full investigation of which has never been completed).The costs to the Lebanese economy were estimated at $6 billion.

In 2008 Hizbollah fighters swept through West Beirut to avenge decisions taken by their Prime Minister Hariri that sought to change their position and prerogatives at the airport in Lebanon by removing all their telecom networks.

In 2018 a major crisis was averted when Israel discovered tunnels allegedly dug by Hizbollah between Lebanon and Israel.

Islamic fundamentalism also created chaos in Northern Lebanon this time. A long and bloody fight took place between the Lebanese Armed Forces and Fateh Al Islam-and the Islamist militant group. It lasted four months in 2008 with numerous casualties on both sides

The net effects of this brief historical review are that Lebanon does have a central government that is constrained by too many contending forces within Lebanon buffeted by many interests and interferences from potent troops outside the country. An excellent example of the latter is the civil war in Syria lasting six years (2011-2017). Two million refugees from Syria drifted into Lebanon, creating massive pressures on the government in terms of health care, housing, security, and education.

But direct and intentional actions by the foreign governments also affect the ability of the Lebanese government to function with clarity and decisiveness. An outrageous example of such was the "house arrest "of Prime Minister Saad Hariri in Saudi Arabia while serving as Prime Minister of Lebanon.

Some today are still arguing, alarmingly, for giving Lebanese nationality cards to these refugees and the 400,000 Palestinians still living in camps in Southern Lebanon. No issue is more controversial!?? This could destroy the character of the state, including the religious distributions in Lebanon.

Confessionalism has not served Lebanon well at all. Some estimated that cronyism in the name of religion and to protect religious perks have cost the Lebanese economy 9% of their GDP. In an experiment conducted by The Lebanese Center for Policy Studies: "70 percent of respondents wanted it to be abolished". But none of them would walk the streets to demonstrate for this position.

In a nutshell, the history of Lebanon is filled with tragedies, natural, and manufactured obstacles that prevent the state from fulfilling its obligation to the people. When all communities and interest groups were pulling the country in different directions, the ship of state is unsteady, and the negative results become very predictable. The possibility of consensus is seriously undermined.

Add to this the hair raising appointments that are made at the highest level of government where the qualifications and ethics of the appointed Minister or top manager are seriously in question, and the possibility of an efficient government is destroyed.

A note on the un-civil, treacherous civil war

The dark period of 1975-1990 was filled with criminality, absurdities, vicious conduct on all sides, inhumanity, and decisions that suffocated any concept of state and national cohesion. Lebanon was a fragmented country with forces that are Lebanese, forces that were foreign but in Lebanon, and forces that sought the dissolution of Lebanon as a state. Each claimed territorial autonomy within zones of influence in Lebanon with 'borders' that were terrorizing to cross. Those zones invariably represented religion and /or some vision for the country. They were run by militias that only understood the power of the gun and became indifferent to the mayhem they were creating in the country. They imposed their own form of taxation, their own system of justice, and lived by dealing in everything, legal and illegal, smuggled arms and drugs, and used extortion when necessary to support their vision. Suddenly nationalism has a new form unlike any the world has known.

Billions were lost, over one hundreds of thousands were killed, over a million people displaced, and the country was in ruin. With all sides exhausted from years of war, the Syrians made their move in October of 1990 when their forces in Lebanon attacked the forces of General Aoun by air and land and forced him into exile.

Putting the country together after so many years of war was very challenging. There were compromises on everything to include the true sovereignty of the state. The Shia population made their deals with Iran, the Sunnis looked for political and financial cover from Saudi Arabia, and the Christians looked westwards. The public square never became a focus for a national dialogue on how to build a civil society that protects the rights of all citizens, how the national wealth is used to benefit all regions of Lebanon, and where true justice is practiced within a democratic framework that ensures honest elections and the rights of every citizen.

We now look at severe cases of abuse and Corruption in the Lebanese economic arena.

Some lessons in Corruption- the Lebanese Way

The cases we discuss in this chapter are symptomatic of the range of corrupt practices that often defy credulity. The documented stories about the airplane leases by Middle Eastern Airlines, the structured Corruption at the port of Beirut, and the old stories about so-called "waste management" are numerous enough to require another book. We recommend a great book by Reinoud Leenders titled *"Spoils of Truce."*

We begin here with the first major crisis in the Lebanese banking sector that involved intrigues at the highest of level, irresponsible banking practices, unwise actions by the new central bank, religious and nationality differences interfering in decent governance, the use of banking resources as one's own, political elites exercising their power when denied access to special consideration, regional political influences, and severe losses for small depositors.

I speak of the collapse of Intra Bank, the largest bank in Lebanon at the time, with 16% of banking deposits in Lebanon.

The story of Intra Bank revolved around a banker by the name of Yusuf Beidas, a Palestinian (mother and wife were both Lebanese) Greek Orthodox. They set up financial operations in Lebanon in 1951.

From a money changer, he became the principal owner of Intra Bank with 19,000 depositors and controlling interests in the Port of Beirut, Middle East Airlines, Lebanon's Casino, and many major hotels. The bank quickly became multinational with offices in Arab Capitals, Brazil and Sierra Leone, London, Paris, and New York.

In 1966 rumors had started circulating that the bank was insolvent: no longer able to meet its financial obligations to its lenders (depositors). By October 15, Intra Bank closed its doors. It did not declare bankruptcy, however.

At the time, the viability of the Lebanese banking system was questioned as the ire of depositors was expressed everywhere.

Price Waterhouse was hired to audit the books. It concluded that the bank was indeed solvent but had a severe liquidity problem. Parenthetically, most Lebanese banks had a similar problem. They could not sustain a rush of withdrawals. In the United States, banks are carefully monitored to make sure that they possess adequate liquidity at all times and that their balance sheets are sufficiently diversified as not to create a risk to depositors and owners. When in need of liquidity, they borrow money in the Fed Funds market, or acquire it through the discount window of the Federal Reserve, issue Commercial Paper, or sell some assets. These measures were not available within the Lebanese banking system.

The Monetary Law of 1963 set up the central bank of Lebanon (Banque du Liban (BDL)) with the expectation that all its regulatory powers will be light. Therefore, the ability of BDL to support Intra bank was still limited. Now they are substantial. BDL could have loaned the needed funds to reassure depositors. After much negotiation, it did and loaned Intra Bank 15 million dollars. The need was for at least $50 million.

Most of the avenues available to the U.S and European banks facing a liquidity crisis were not available to Intra Bank despite its ownership of the prime real estate in Lebanon, Paris, London, New York, and other countries.

Adding to the illiquidity of assets were two factors:
1- The development of the Eurodollar market, based in London, promising secured bonds at much higher interest rates. Arab depositors in Lebanon rushed to cash in, thus decreasing the liquidity of Intra bank.
2- Mr. Beidas seemed to have alienated the political class and the economic elite in Lebanon that was mostly Maronite and Sunni. They sat on the sideline, watching the bank sink deeper. They could have bought more shares in the bank, thereby infusing considerable liquidity. Unable to sell shares or substantial assets, the bank was restructured. Some of its assets were taken over by a new Bank: El Mashrek and some of its creditors became shareholders in a new company: Intra Investment. The Lebanese government approved a budget to compensate for the small depositors. All directors were jailed. The Lebanese cabinet denied any bailout funds and did permit the bank to reopen under the previous management and business model.

The consequences of the years of turmoil caused by Intra bank were a fall in Lebanon's GDP growth and a tarnished image for Lebanon as a banking center.

The tragedy of Intra Bank illustrated the caustic interaction between politics and finance and the inclusion of the political/economic elite in the spoils of the system, especially when their "share" is not preserved.

We now look at Solidere as a manifestation of their political power over a massive real estate project with the newly conceived interpretation of property rights.

Solidere

It is 1990, and the Taef Agreement became fully effective. The center of Beirut was in ruins. All buildings were battle scared and, in many cases, totally irredeemable. The Center of Beirut was empty except for rats and rubbish-strewn streets that were mostly impassible. A massive reconstruction effort was called for as Beirut had to be revived as a symbol of new horizons for Lebanon. It had to be, once again, the heart of the Lebanese economy and its political system.

The Prime Minister at the time was Rafiq Hariri- a construction tycoon with vast wealth originating from his businesses in Saudi Arabia and elsewhere.

He was, realistically, faced with daunting dilemmas relating to property laws in Lebanon, especially concerning the rights of renters, as he had sought out to rebuild Beirut. Lebanese laws do not allow landlords to evict renters without compensation. That sum could exceed the value of the property, and the renter can still say no. The challenge, therefore, was to be fair to the renters and the property owners. That required massive legislation to supersede existing laws. Hariri's answer was to build a partnership with the Lebanese government that allows Solidere to use the power of eminent domain with a mandate to manage the center of Beirut. The area covered about 200 hectares. More was added to the area when the seafront was expanded, creating what is now called Zaitouneh Bay.

Meantime architects from all over the world were hard at work, developing a master plan and parts. Among them, Dar Al Handasa, Zaha Hadid, Steven Holl from the US, Angus Gavin (U.K.), Rafael Moneo (Spain), Giancarlo de Carlo (Italy), Peter Marino (U.S.), etc.

The holistic and ambitious designs then became a requirement for all landowners to abide by to make sure that the vision the new downtown for Beirut is executed correctly within a specific time framework.

Solidere was organized as a corporate entity. Its shares were traded on the Beirut Stock Exchange as Global Depository Receipts.

The execution of this huge project required an assessment of the value of each property in relation to the share value set at $10. That is, if the cost of a property is deemed by the experts at Solidere to be worth $10,000,000, you will receive 1 million shares. The share price after that was to be determined by market forces. No shareholder could own more than ten percent of Solidere (a highly disputed amount with regard to the Hariri holdings).

Three factors created a controversy that still has currency today:

1- The property owner was offered from the following: take the shares we have assessed you deserve or build according to specifications in our grand design and within a specified period and meet all the standards. No financing of any kind was offered to the property owner. Almost all property owners felt that the choice is only to take the shares, unfair as the price was deemed to be.

2- The plan requires special legislation. Mr. Hariri was Prime Minister. He needed to make sure that all the wheels were appropriately greased. Numerous stories were told about bribes and exclusive deals. We were not able to confirm their nature and extent

3- The infrastructure of the wise entire downtown required development. $20 billion of construction money was to be spent to meet the design requirements. Solidere had made a deal with the Lebanese government where Hariri was the Prime Minister to rebuild the infrastructure of the downtown Beirut area (something Solidere had to do anyway to make sure their buildings were fully operational, efficient and marketable) in exchange for an area called Normandy which includes what is now referred to as Zeitouni Bay (easily the most expensive real estate in Lebanon today). The Normandy area was created through the excavation of the Mediterranean Sea in that zone. In this, Mr. Hariri realized the ultimate deal.

No property owner, the author discussed Solidere with felt that the offer was fair. One characterized it as a "mafia-style offer." One previous owner yearned for the beauty of his property and wished that he didn't have to accept the settlement.

The Corruption involved in the process was simply "necessary," one commentator argued as that is the way Lebanon "works." How scandalous!

Now we look at the latest scheme to destroy trust and with

it the image of a country.

The Land of Milk and Honey- Its image and economy destroyed

Lebanon produces an oversupply of many doctors and engineers and sends them to solve certain environmental and medical problems all around the world. This has been the case since engineers from Tyre built Carthage, a magnificent city that rivaled Rome.

The environmental engineers and the electrical engineers in Lebanon have been co-opted and corrupted by the political class, which lives off favors and by keeping its hands in the public purse. Twenty-four-hour electricity still is not ordinary in Lebanon, whose engineers worked on lighting up most of the Arab world and much of Africa and now stand helpless to solve another embarrassing crisis. The national electricity deficit in Lebanon has been covered by privately-owned generators selling electricity to households whose electricity has been interrupted (while still paying the monthly subscription to the government) or by private ownership of generators with attending accidents and trips to the hospitals or even death. A new lobby of generator owners emerged to lobby on their behalf and prevent a return to 24-hour electricity provided by the central government. This entity loses about one billion dollars a year (some say 2 billion), adding to the budget deficit, and its equipment is antiquated. Instead of revamping the system, the former Minister of energy, Gebran Basil proposed paying "a Turkish company $1.9 billion for power "that would be generated from Turkish barges off the coast of Lebanon (N.Y. Times December 3, 2019).

Known as The Switzerland of the Middle East, Lebanon has also been traditionally called, continued to experience a garbage crisis that became a health hazard, as well as an environmental hazard and a total disaster for the image of Lebanon as a tourist country. It started in 2015 and witnessed an incredible series of protests, some with severe violence. All types of waste to include medical and chemical waste littered Beirut's streets and its beaches: "The Mediterranean gurgle (d) with Toxic runoffs and rotting garbage" reported N.Y. Times. One fisherman was quoted as saying, "we live in a garbage can."

This is a case of a perfectly dysfunctional government that is refusing to address problems that affect the health and the wellbeing of its citizens. It is a fact that 85 percent of Lebanon's waste goes into open dumps or landfills, but only 10-12 percent of it cannot be "composted or recycled."

Just like in the areas that we have addressed above, crony sectarianism perpetrated the crisis. New landfills were being opened with ownership going to the protégé of a politician:

A $288 million contract for a landfill went to "Jihad al Arab," whose brother is connected to PM Hariri. Another Landfill in a different Zone went to "Dany Khoury" whose family is close to Michel Aoun, the current President of Lebanon. It was alleged that "at this landfill experts found employees dumped trash and their toxic waste directly into

the Mediterranean "(The NY Times, 12/ 3/ 2019).
Numerous more incidents of Corruption were reported by Reinoud Leenders in his book: Spoils of Truce, Corruption in Post War Lebanon, published in Cornell Press 2012.
These documented and exposed acts of Corruption have not diminished Corruption at all in Lebanon. The fact that none of the abusers was identified and prosecuted encouraged further Corruption. Files are opened to investigate and to prosecute. Suddenly, they are closed, and the abuser is smoking fat cigars in the plush cafes of Beirut.
We now look at the latest scheme to destroy trust and appropriate public wealth to select oligarchs instead of using massive resources to solve fundamental economic problems, improve the environment, run an efficient state and stabilize the national currency.

How to Rob a country of its newly discovered Energy Source

Lebanon is blessed, as it turns out, by enormous oil and gas deposits. The reserves are located in what is referred to as the Levant Basin. It's estimated that the basin contains 122 trillion cubic feet of natural gas and 1.7 billion barrels of recoverable oil. It is also estimated that the recoverable gas reserves are 25 trillion cubic feet. Many oil companies from France, Italy, Russia, Malaysia, and the U.K. have shown great interest. No oil or gas has been produced as yet after years of study and negotiations. However, preparations and numerous studies have been made to include the

administrative structure for oil and gas in Lebanon.
The current Administrative structure (set up on December 4, 2012) by the Ministry of Energy and Water is called:
The Lebanese Petroleum Administration (LPA).
It is made up of six members appointed by the Minister (religious distribution is observed)

Here are the Pronounced Anomalies:

1-The law that set up the structure expired but was extended by Prime Minister Hariri. The relevant law is: Article number 5 of the 43rd Decree
2-All the oil-producing countries (over 70) own national companies involved in the extraction and production of oil. Lebanon DOES NOT.
3- Typically, the revenue for oil is a split 40% for the government and the rest for the oil company. Not in the case of Lebanon. Lebanon receives NO participation share in its first licensing round.
This was in full violation of the Offshore Petroleum Resources Law.
4- Two Categories of companies were defined:

A- Operators: Doing the actual work of extraction and production.

B- Non-operators: Uniquely structured in an incredible Lebanese scheme.

5- The LPA approved 53 companies, most of which were

FAKE companies. One of these companies "is based on Hong Kong with a total capital of $1,300 belonging to a Lebanese politician."

6- The Scheme devised by the LPA.

-"A legitimate world-class operator company requests to work in Lebanon."

- "the LPA approves the request on one condition: The operator must be accompanied by two non-operating (shadow (fake) companies that claim about ten percent of the profit.'

The government gets nothing in the first round. It can only appoint a Lebanese supervisor to supervise the operating companies.

The disaster that this twisted arrangement represents is as follows:

- Pollution in Lebanon will continue as many countries have already switched to natural gas-powered cars.
- The electricity production in Lebanon will remain expensive, unreliable, and a great source of Corruption.
- The national debt will continue to accumulate. Oil was supposed to be a critical solution to the debt crisis.

Rome (Beirut) is burning

What makes the situation further compelling is the fact that Lebanon does not have intellectual properties to export in terms of new frontiers in technology, primary research, and A.I. developments. Its engineers and scientists are creating high-value exports for other countries. It relies upon the exports of pearls and precious stones, machinery and electrical instruments, prepared foodstuff, beverages and tobacco, products of the chemical and allied industries, base metals and articles of base metals, vegetable products, plastic, rubber and articles thereof, the pulp of wood, paper and paper board, miscellaneous manufactured articles, animal or vegetable fats, and oils.

We mention these meager exports because Lebanon imports everything else to include a total of 120,000 barrels of oil daily. Yet, it is in no hurry to export its gas and oil and stop oil imports.

Israel, with less oil and gas resources, is already self-sufficient in energy. Lebanon needs to immediately embark on responsible and efficient oil exploration to reduce its trade deficit, which is currently at about $15 billion a year. This will translate into less reliance on remittances, will reduce environmental degradation as cars and electricity will be powered by natural gas, and will certainly stabilize the national currency.

The perennial question is asked once again: will the Political elite allow Accepted economic rationality to prevail in Lebanon?

Conclusion

The days of political reform have come and gone. The current system must be abandoned in favor of one where scientific planning and execution, character, and competency matter. Those who have systematically stolen from the public purse must be prosecuted, so a lesson for the younger generation is transmitted.

Chapter 3
The Lebanese Economy: A Broader View

Introduction

No people on the face of the earth have had a more global view and urgency to travel to every corner of the world in search of opportunities than the Lebanese and their ancestors. One need not go back to Carthage (9th Century B.C.) to become convinced of this. The Lebanese are everywhere, and they are still discovering new places to go to. It is surprising that the first man that landed on the moon was not Lebanese. Or was he?

The Lebanese have always looked beyond the immediate horizon and always saw an opportunity. He traded, preached, cajoled, set up enterprises, peddled, and invented. His personal journey through the globe was a warlike struggle, but he prevailed nonetheless. The path was set by his ancestors, who created the multinational corporation and the alphabet: two critical engines for world growth.

There are at least four times of Lebanese residing overseas than in Lebanon. But not all of their hearts have left Lebanon. This very fact and their actions account for much of Lebanon's growth, the general economic stability Lebanon enjoyed, and the success of the "rescue missions" to stabilize the economy when disasters struck.

Their economic and associated political powers in numerous countries far exceed those of any ethnic group, including Jewish groups in some countries. They have demonstrated themselves as gifted individuals as God has ever created. But, on a collective level, they remain a work in progress.

Just ask the Japanese whose country has no natural resources that explain their industrial successes. Building a nation is not just about individual talent and resources. It is also about excellent planning, entrepreneurship, organization, social cohesion, self-reliance, good political leadership, a shared sense of purpose all exercised in a democratic context where everyone is equal before the law.

There simply isn't any economic, scientific, intellectual, or social ladder that the immigrant Lebanese has not successfully climbed. They are overrepresented in many fields, such as medicine, business, and politics. But they still yearn for Lebanon, thankfully!

It's said that "You can take the boy out of the country, but cannot take the country out of the boy."

Now for some serious economic discussion!

The immigrant Lebanese and their descendants have vested Lebanon with:

- Economic capital.
- Political capital.
- Entrepreneurial capital.
- Emotional capital.
- Intellectual capital.
- Global trading capital.
- Cultural and religious capitals.
- Knowledge capital, and so on.

In fact, there is no way the citizens of Lebanon can live the way they do without these vested capitals. The massive trade deficit Lebanon incurs annually with exports covering only 16% of the imports, and the large annual budget deficit (15.3 % of GDP in 2020) of the revenue are the constant irritants to Lebanon's growth and its economic stability. Unfortunately, even when services and net unilateral transfers are added, the Current Account Balance remained negative in some years, as we demonstrate below. Lebanon will continue to depend on international support as its inadequate currency regime, spending priorities, lagging exports, political Corruption, economic policies, cronyism, the under-exercised of the massive intellectual capacity of its people in a worldwide knowledge economy, and Corruption continue.

Arab Gulf countries have given considerable support for Lebanon in terms of grants, loans, and direct investment. The European Union and the United States have also been generous with Lebanon. But it never seemed enough:

The United States government was the top donor of the year 2018, and invested 494,293,328 dollars in critical water and sanitation infrastructure, creating opportunities for the Lebanese citizens, agriculture, and businesses, assisting host communities and meeting the basic needs of so many vulnerable refugees and Lebanese, improving schools and providing scholarships for the students, and building the capacity of Lebanese primary health clinics, hospitals and municipalities.

Since 2007, the United States has provided more than $4.8 billion in total combined assistance to Lebanon, including more than $1.7 billion in military aid and more than $3.1 billion in development and humanitarian assistance.

International rescue packages were rather generous to Lebanon and offered much solace to its citizens. But it did not cure its fundamental political and economic ills. There was Paris I, Paris II (commitments of $4.4 billion for Lebanon from twelve countries and five international organizations), The Stockholm conference (allowing Lebanon to raise $896 million in grants and soft loans. 40 governments and 20 international Institutions were involved), and Paris III ($3.7 billion were effectively received by December 2009. $3.48 billion were committed to project financing. $1.74 billion to support the budget of the Lebanese government and $1.46 billion to support the private sector, plus more).

Where did the money go? Was Lebanon stabilized in the long run?

By 2020 Lebanon appears to be on the brink of an economic collapse.

We now consider why, based on well-known economic principles. We focus first on the Balance of Payments deficit.

The Persistent Balance of Payments Deficit

The Balance of Payments deficits, particularly the Current Account deficits, and the budget deficits are the twin towers that do not cease to irritate and to threaten the economic health of Lebanon.

As is typically the case, these deficits are covered by:

- Capital flows.

- Remittances.
- Flows associated with Direct Investment.
- External borrowing, and when in crisis.
- Liquidation of gold reserves, if any, or using accumulated dollar reserves in the Central Bank.

There is no way the Lebanese economy can function and keep up the standard of living of the Lebanese without such capital inflows. The solvency of the Lebanese state, unfortunately, depends on massive borrowing from overseas funded in part by the immigrants. The total debt of Lebanon had reached $85 billion (150% of GDP) by the end of 2019, and there is no end in sight for its continued growth. Lebanon borrows to pay deficits, pay the debt due, and pay interest on the debt.

A simple primer on the calculation of the current account should be helpful.

Please note that a surplus in the capital account must finance a deficit in the current account.

We now look at how.

Current Account

X – M ± Unilateral Transfers [gifts, donations, unilateral transfers, REMITTANCES*]

Where

X = Exports = money coming in

M = Imports = money going out

<u>Plus or minus</u> investment income, interest, dividends, rents, and profit income

CAB, the Current account balance is

CAB= X-M + NI (net income) + NCT (net current transfers)
Is negative then
the country is a net debtor
Elements of the Capital Account
1- Foreign Direct Investment
2- Foreign Institutional Investments
3- Borrowing from Abroad
4- Change in Foreign exchange reserves or gold reserves
Persistent current account deficits usher a more significant debt burden and severe instability for the country.
The latest attempt by the Lebanese government to borrow in the International Markets was both luckily and generously deflected in good percentages by the Qatari and the Saudi governments. Still, now there is a new reality that is more fundamental.
In 2018, BOP (Balance of Payments) deficits were extensive by international standards. In October alone, the current account deficit was $1.8 billion, In November, it was $950 million, and in December $747.5 million. The total current account deficit for 2018 was around $15 billion. It should be noted here that there were a few times in the history of Lebanon when the government budget had been in surplus, the last time in 2005, precisely when an honest minister of finance was in office. Therefore, the government revenues are, in theory, sufficient, barring any corruption.
Except for January, all months in 2018 had BOP deficits.
The story repeated itself as it usually does, and the current account deficit in 2019 was $11 billion.

Unless the government is running a sufficiently large standard budget surplus, it will not be able to cover these deficits nor the interest on the accumulated debt. It invariably borrows the money either domestically or internationally, and the accumulated debt inexorably grows.

The total outstanding debt of the Lebanese government stands now at 186.6 % of GDP in 2020, among the highest in the world. Total debt at the end of 2019 stood at $89 billion.

How do you cover such a deficit? And also, how do you cover the budget deficit of almost $4.5 billion (mostly caused by interest on the debt- the primary balance is also in deficit: $600 million).

Remittances are one source and a very important source for Lebanon.

Some economists have estimated that the Lebanese immigrant accounts for about 60% of Lebanon's GDP. Lebanon lives off REMITTANCES from Lebanese living overseas.

Much of this foreign capital hasn't been efficiently utilized. Yes, large real estate projects and deals are executed, but where are the institutions that deal with the infrastructures, where is the fiscal discipline, who is watching over the environmental degradation, and where are the employment opportunities for the numerous graduates that Lebanon produces annually?

The indigenous Lebanese are ever intent on proving their cunning abilities, their superior skills at manipulating different facts and events, their ability to put "self" above the collective interest and the relevance of institutions, as well as their ability to ignore the underlying political trends in the country. The importance of personal cults and securing one's share in the public treasury is somehow an entitlement. The elite appropriate to themselves 100% of the internal political power in Lebanon while denying the majority of Lebanese the true gifts of democracy.

Yet, the typical new immigrant Lebanese will continue to forget, hope, pray, and help on a substantial scale. An increasing number of immigrant Lebanese are dropping out, their interest and connectivity to their homeland is falling, and many are sick and tired of the divisions, the Corruption, and the excuses. The indigenous Lebanese need to pay attention, as the second, the third, and the fourth generation of immigrant Lebanese are ever less forgiving. Lebanon cannot continue to rely on sentimental investments. Money coming back simply because someone wants to show success due to immigration, and some attachment to the land will no longer be the order of the day.

Lebanon must, therefore, pay attention to the classical factors affecting international investment flows:

- Liquidity of the investment.
- Likelihood of interruption in the cash flows and/or issues with currency values and currency convertibility.

- Taxation.
- Risk factors include political risk and business risk.
- Quality and cost of labor.
- Infrastructure and the costs of using it.
- And the contagion effects stemming from operating in a volatile neighborhood where terrorism is on the rise.

We cite a few examples of the desperate need for reforms:

The electricity of Lebanon is probably the best case in this point, and frankly a stark embarrassment. The institution has sucked a huge amount of public money, some state as much as $14 billion, and there are electric shortages and outages and brownouts and blackouts throughout Lebanon. The net current deficit, the annual cost of electricity generation, is estimated at $1.5 billion. This is scandalous and unacceptable. The rumors about what happened to the money are as inventive as the schemes used to defraud the government. Many want the problem to disappear for good. They are late converts to privatization but who would want to acquire an entity saddled with cronyism and bad debt. Many steal electricity, and many steal from the government by not paying their electricity bills.

This franchise has no value, especially when it is regularly losing money (requiring subsidies annually). Adding to these problems is the absence of fiscal enforcement.

The best minds in electricity generation have been consulted. All of Lebanon may have been efficiently electrified for about $2 billion. No one has ever been charged

with a crime relating to the electricity scandal, however.
We referred to the State of California when it experienced energy disruptions in the period 2000 to 2001 to gauge the possibility of stabilizing the electricity generating sector in Lebanon and its costs.
Many factors contributed to the sudden shortage of electricity in the most dynamic economy in the United States. The state decided to create a significant natural gas-powered plant called: The Sutter Energy Center. The plans started in 1999. On July 2, 2001, the plant was inaugurated, producing 540 Megawatts. The cost was $350 million. Lebanon consumes about 21 million megawatts. Four plants similar to the Sutter would suffice for the entire country of Lebanon. The total cost of such would be less than the forecasted $2billion, even accounting for inflation.
The sad thing is that the energy cabal in Lebanon must have been fully aware of such possibilities and their cost.
Had the extraction of the enormous oil and gas reserves in Lebanon been started around the same time as Lebanon's neighbors had, the electricity would have been a huge source of revenue for the government. However, the interminable discussions and planning, and schemes had continued. No lessons had been learned from other countries and their experiences.
The discovery of massive and rather substantial deposits of natural gas in Lebanon was a massive bonanza. Four power stations in the various corners of Lebanon powered by gas, the marginal cost of which is almost zero, could have been

installed. The life, prosperity, and welfare of every Lebanese would have been enhanced at a much lower cost. Energy-intensive industries would be attracted to Lebanon.

One must realize that the majority of the current debt in Lebanon is all accumulated interest. Lebanon now has the distinction of being one of the top three most heavily indebted countries per capita in the world. The debt may have risen since this book project started.

Recently, the Lebanese banks started massive marketing campaigns to pull dollars into the country at remarkably high-interest rates of up to 15 percent on a five-year term Lebanese pound deposits, with minimum deposits ranging from $20,000 to $50,000.

Other offers reported by Reuters included 10 percent on one-year and 11 percent on two-year terms, with minimum deposits ranging from $20,000 to up to $50,000.

Ask yourselves why these high-interest rates are being offered. The critical answer is political risk and Corruption. Adding to the concerns of International Investors is the lowering of Lebanon's credit rating one level to Caa1 by Moody's Investors Service. This translates into a credit rating below the junk category.

Privatization, should it take place today, would buy time, but will not rescue the country. Lebanon has received plenty of help and advice from all over the world. The problem is that the rest of the world is not on a Lebanese clock and cannot forever wait for the 'collective' ears of the Lebanese to begin listening. The World Bank, the IMF, the American

Government, Paris I, Paris II, and III spoke of the need to privatize some key industries. Lebanon did not, and the required fiscal discipline is still elusive.

Using taxes as the mechanism for addressing the continuing economic problems is not the answer. The indigenous Lebanese have forgotten their roots and their source of prosperity when it comes to taxes. No country ever achieved long term prosperity due to excessive taxation. The tax burden in Lebanon is excessive. This discourages investments and ends up reducing the tax collections by the government. Yet, there are ever more cries and plans for more taxation. The VAT tax was implemented, and a host of taxes on investment and energy were introduced to adjust the salaries of public employees and meet debt payments. This is the French model, and look at what it got France.

The American model relies on the reduction of taxes. This has increased tax collection in the U.S. The tax collection process, and its effects are straight forward. In 2006 taxes were lowered in the U.S. Tax collections jumped by 13.5%. The formula is simple: lower taxes increase economic growth and INCREASE government revenue (IBN Khaldoun- not really Laffer). This economic reality, combined with fiscal discipline, produce long- term economic growth and stability.

It must be kept in mind that the worst and most regressive tax of all is corruption. The poor are unable to escape it.

The political division and the constant political paralysis have led many people in Washington to wonder if there is anything the Lebanese people can agree on. There is not a single national issue that the Lebanese may have a common stand on, or so it seems to the outsider. Instead of arguing about how to distribute the national pie, the Lebanese should agree on mechanisms for increasing the size of the pie so all the Lebanese will prosper.

The immigrants need to know what to sell in Washington and elsewhere without looking as foolish and contradictory.

Other Issues Affecting Economic Performance

The environment: Many of us left Lebanon as that oasis by the Mediterranean, only to come back to a country where 80% of its groundwater is polluted according to the World Bank, the air that is not breathable in the summer, and some beaches that would actually be closed in many countries of the world.

Just walk on the beach as you watch the filth floating on Lebanon's shores. The garbage collection issue that festered for two years has been a genuine embarrassment. This is unforgivable. Its effects on tourism are significant.

The world couldn't believe what goes on and how things are done in Lebanon. The Garbage Crisis, as well as the general environmental degradation in Lebanon, have sullied the reputation of Lebanon and especially the status of its politicians. The underlying corruption was exposed for everyone to see. None of what happened is excusable.

On the education front, Lebanon is slipping even in the

regional ranking. Despite considerable assistance from the U.S and other governments, and massive contributions to many higher education institutions in Lebanon, Lebanon has yet to develop a first-rate university based on excellence in fields of research. I am not aware of any university where basic research is ongoing. Many continue to try, but the battle is hard and long indeed. India often and erroneously referred to as 'poor India," has already produced universities that are harder to get into than Harvard. They are leaders in technology and software development.

Lebanon can do just as well. World economic development is more knowledge-based than ever before.

Lebanon can play a major part, but it has been, instead, a major exporter of brainpower. No citizen is more endowed by his creator than the Lebanese. We can become a research and development center for the world. To do so, you must listen more, and you must learn from the collective experiences of the immigrant Lebanese.

You must also remove the suffocating bureaucratic red tape, and the most hideous tax of all: corruption. The evidence suggests that Lebanon has been retreating on the higher education front. In Engineering, the top Lebanese university is ranked 17th in the Arab World.

Lebanese students were ranked 58th in reading, science, and math in 2015. These are not the bases for creating a country that is a learning center for its citizens and for the Arab World.

All the money in the world couldn't create a new Google in

Lebanon. Intellectual capital and commitment to basic research, legal protections, political stability, and accountability are essential to economic growth.

Conclusions

Lebanese immigrants are counting on the indigenous Lebanese to stop political bickering, start talking to instead of at each other, set an honorable and sustainable political-economic agenda, and prosecute those that seek to undermine, if not disrupt the public will and good. Expats will help the indigenous Lebanese understand and benefit in a new world with China bidding to lead it, and in which your fellow Latinos, (most Lebanese in the world are citizens of Latin countries) are playing ever more critical roles. In the U.S. today, 60% of all births in many cities are to Latin parents. This will have a transforming effect on the American economy as well as the American foreign policy. The immigrant Lebanese know their language. They also know how to get Brazil, for example, to understand and support Lebanon.

There is no reason why Lebanon cannot become a center for higher education, software development, car design, and high fashion as Mr. Elie Saab and as several others have demonstrated. Genius and creativity are indeed exportable and have global value. The Lebanese could focus on money management, consultancy on economic, financial, and architectural issues in the Middle East and beyond, and the creation of a major center for medical tourism. These efforts can pay enormous dividends.

For these seeds to grow, we have to create a nurturing environment. It all starts with political stability, good governance, and the reduction of corrupt practices.

Should all the Lebanese talent produced in Lebanon to stay at home, Lebanon could break that glass ceiling of entrepreneurship, innovation, and the export of intellectually-based products and services. The world could expect the next Uber or Instagram, or other new horizons in money management to come out of this newly formed Lebanon.

The energy reserves of Lebanon will supplant this technology base if aggressively and competently managed.

The energy resources are valued at one trillion dollars, which is more than 100 times the national debt, with vast reserves of funds left to develop the most modern and comprehensive infrastructure in the world.

Should these recommendations not be implemented, plus an actual crisis results, the 20.8 Billion in the Banque du Liban and the $11.5 billion in gold will simply not be enough to correct course.

Lebanon will do well to heed the lessons learned by Ireland, a country with a similar size population, and a huge number of citizens who migrated throughout the world, the United States especially. Twenty-two U.S. Presidents are of Irish descent. The 2008 financial crisis almost broke the back of Ireland. But working together and innovatively, they are now prospering.

Ireland has risen to become a significant attraction for world business interested in expanding the frontiers of technology. It's the banking system, and regulatory structures are pretty sound and attractive. Its austerity program and lower taxes are paying off handsomely.

Its colleges are expanding, and its innovation district is also thriving. Many banks are moving their headquarters from London to Dublin; Google hired 1,000 employees in Ireland for CLOUD computing, Microsoft has 2,200 employees, Facebook has 4,000 employees, and so on. Today Ireland is considered the most open economy after Singapore.

Lebanon produces a lot of brainpower. The best way to keep them in the country is for politicians to keep their hands off of the political/ budget jar (Lebanon is 136th in the world on the Corruption Index along with Kyrgyzstan, Myanmar, Nigeria, and Papua New Guinea), bring the infrastructure to world standards, eliminate unnecessary regulations, reform the justice system to reduce its dependence on politics, and begin producing clean energy that would remove much of the pollution in Lebanon [Cars converted to natural gas power] and will cut the cost of electricity very substantially.

Bound by a shared destiny, with good government and solid, unifying, non-sectarian plans, Lebanon could become that "Shining City on the Hill'.

Chapter 4
The Seeds of the 2020 Crisis

Special acknowledgment
This chapter received considerable contributions (especially for the graphs and tables) from Dr. Poorna Pal. I owe him much gratitude for his work.

Introduction

The financial Tsunami that is currently devastating Lebanon and impoverishing its citizens has been forming since the early 1990s. This chapter looks at the seeds that were planted along the way and generated the destructive forces now threatening every aspect of the nation's life: business entities are failing, malls are closing, plummeting currency value, negative economic growth, environmental degradation, massive public unrest, government locking out depositors in the banking system, sizeable outward immigration, etc.

This scenario marks the underlying catastrophe that resulted from inept and unscrupulous economic policies and severe structural problems in Lebanon's economy. Lebanon's financial meltdown and civic rage now threaten all the institutions in Lebanon and the very viability of the state. In this chapter, we explore the economic factors and policies (e.g., austerity, political corruption, recession, sectarianism, unemployment, etc.) as well as the role that the Lebanese central bank (BDL) played in disrupting the life of every Lebanese.

Economic factors and policies:

We examine the economic factors and misguided policies as an explanation for the 2020 crisis. This crisis is essentially a governance crisis that emanated from the broken sectarian system that stalled rational policymaking and allowed a culture of corruption, nepotism, government jobs as political payoffs, and waste.

Lebanon's historically fragile government has depended on increasing public debt to square its payments while failing to implement reforms that could have invigorated the economy and increased international investments. Instead, public debt continued to accumulate as the government was not even able to pay the interest on the debt. That interest had to be capitalized.

This turned Lebanon into the third most indebted state in the world. Rampant corruption has further depleted the national treasury and added to the debt burden. Inexorably, the debt increase has produced the burden of growing interest service. Such large and growing annual financing needs have made the country increasingly vulnerable to external shocks.

As external financial flows into Lebanon slowed, the central bank resorted to desperate and extreme efforts to attract dollar deposits to maintain the currency peg (1507LL/$) and to finance government purchases.

Ultimately, this proved unsustainable. Since October 2019, Lebanon experienced a virtual cessation of capital inflows and a sharp acceleration of outflows. Table 4.1 summarizes some of these data. Of note is the curious and very substantial increase in GDP in 2007- 2010 as the world was suffering from a recession caused by a financial crisis. Lebanon is one of the middle-income countries that has clearly been living beyond her means, but the temporary reprieve did not last.

	GDP		per capita GDP		Exports of goods and services (% of GDP)	External balance on goods and services (% of GDP)	External debt stocks (% of GNI)
	Billion Current US $	Annual Growth (%)	Current US $	Annual Growth (%)			
2000	17.26	1.34	4491.64	-1.16	14.18	-21.76	57.31
2001	17.65	3.84	4422.39	-0.02	15.60	-24.35	77.06
2002	19.15	3.42	4579.46	-1.31	16.10	-18.85	95.77
2003	20.08	3.23	4576.39	-1.62	16.74	-20.62	113.59
2004	21.15	6.29	4627.66	2.08	35.73	-20.38	112.13
2005	21.49	2.75	4573.54	-0.08	37.30	-19.02	107.04
2006	22.05	1.70	4632.31	0.40	36.14	-19.43	109.13
2007	24.87	9.34	5217.47	9.17	37.64	-23.23	101.19
2008	29.23	9.25	6134.13	9.31	38.97	-29.01	148.41
2009	35.48	10.05	7371.10	8.95	33.70	-23.51	130.90
2010	38.42	8.04	7756.74	4.98	35.79	-24.44	126.14
2011	40.08	0.92	7703.39	-3.92	36.94	-27.24	124.67
2012	44.23	2.72	7985.85	-3.52	34.48	-25.72	126.57
2013	46.87	2.62	7923.85	-3.90	31.82	-25.62	133.14
2014	48.30	1.88	7712.06	-3.77	27.85	-26.22	134.83
2015	49.97	0.42	7649.83	-3.74	27.32	-19.48	136.88
2016	51.24	1.61	7634.95	-1.10	25.27	-21.48	139.98
2017	53.39	0.55	7838.34	-0.94	23.85	-24.79	138.68
2018	56.64	0.20	8269.79	-0.34	23.34	-16.27	145.11

Table 4.1: GDP (Gross Domestic Product) and related economic statistics for Lebanon (Source: World Development Indicators database accessed on May 28, 2020)

Add to this dire over-indebtedness situation, the gradual cessation of remittances from abroad, and we can well imagine how the country has become increasingly ungovernable. Lebanon is, of course, a middle-income country in the Arab world and, based on the 2011 World Bank data on --inequitable the wealth distribution---is, Lebanon's Gini coefficient of 37.1 places it right in the middle of the comity of nations worldwide.

But a better index to capture this statistic is the "Human Development Index" (HDI) developed by the United Nations Development Program (UNDP). It is the geometric mean of normalized indices for each of the three dimensions: a long and healthy life, being knowledgeable, and a decent standard of living. As Figure 4.1 shows, this index places Lebanon right in the middle of the comity of nations.

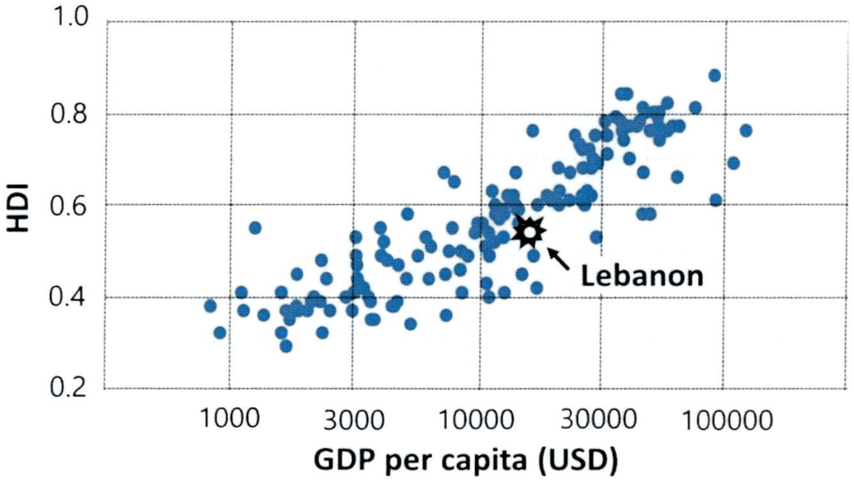

Figure 4.1: Comparing Lebanon's human development index with other countries

But that situation has deteriorated over the past decade and, as the comparison of time series of HDI data for Lebanon with the corresponding mean data for the Arab States and the whole World as Figure 4.2 shows, Lebanon used to be placed far better than the world's average until about 5-6 years ago.

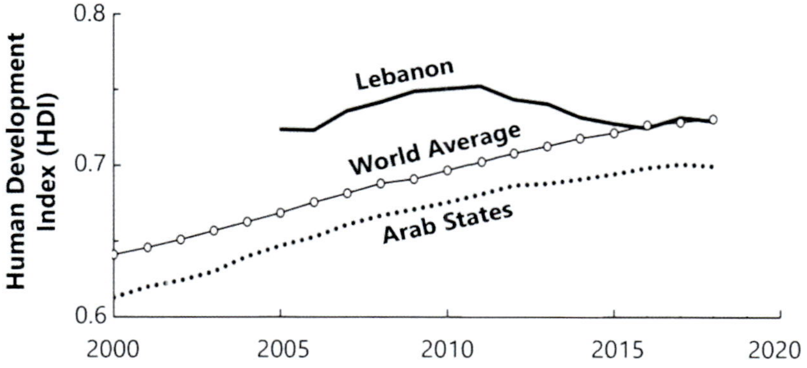

Figure 4.2: Comparing Lebanon's human development index with the corresponding mean HDI data for the world and the Arab States. (Source: http://hdr.undp.org/en/data accessed on 6/12/2020)

Notice the significant drop in Lebanon's HDI between 2010 and 2015! This clearly reflects a comprehensive decline in all ----------Lebanese living conditions that are vital to a modern society's socio-economic survival. The drop encompasses the factors ranging from longevity and health to learning, knowledge, and professional skills on the one hand and the economy and the living standards on the other. Earlier, the Lebanese citizens had enjoyed those conditions prevalent in middle income to richer countries. They now live at the level of the world-average. Surely, this doesn't speak of horrific conditions, except that such rapid declines tend to be the harbingers of intense socio-economic upheavals.

As for the specific measures that matter, the UNDP has identified that, for countries in the higher income bracket, the Gini index correlates the most with the informality of business, and with SB time (average Number of days needed to start a business). Figure 4.3 shows the correlation matrix of these characteristics. This matrix shows robust correlations ($0.5 \leq |r|$ where r is the linear correlation coefficient) between these characteristics:

(a) The Gini index correlates strongly and positively with an average number of days needed to start a business and informality or the percentage of firms competing with unregistered firms);

(b) GDP per capita correlates strongly positively with Transparency International's corruption perception index (the higher the transparency, the more positive the index); and

(c) World Bank Doing Business Ranking has a strong positive correlation with an average number of days needed to start a business, the cost of starting a business as a percent of per capita income, enforcement of contracts, and the ease of getting credit.

The same UNDP report also found that, for economically poor or less developed countries, strong correlations exist between GDP per capita and DB, SB cost, Credit and Manufacturing, and education.

Thus, the deterioration in Lebanon's HDI rating seen in Figure 4.2 clearly reflects rises in time and costs needed for a business to start, increase in the perception of corruption, greater laxity in enforcement of contracts, and difficulties in getting credit for the business.

The immediate source of this state of affairs and Lebanon's resulting socio-economic dysfunction is financial at its core.

Table 4.2 shows how and why profligate spending and living beyond her means have been the culprit here. Note how negative has Lebanon's current account balance been. Since 2012, it has consistently stayed above one fifth of the country's GDP, except for one year.

	Current account balance		External balance on goods and services		Debt service on external debt, total	
	(bill US $)	(% of GDP)	(bill US $)	(% of GDP)	(bill US $)	(% of GDP)
2000	–	–	-3.76	-21.76	1.49	8.64
2001	–	–	-4.30	-24.35	1.49	8.45
2002	-4.18	-23.71	-3.61	-18.85	2.22	11.60
2003	-4.90	-25.59	-4.14	-20.62	3.34	16.63
2004	-4.18	-20.83	-4.31	-20.38	4.46	21.09
2005	-2.70	-12.79	-4.09	-19.02	3.63	16.91
2006	-1.09	-5.06	-4.28	-19.43	4.52	20.51
2007	-1.42	-6.45	-5.78	-23.23	4.76	19.12
2008	-3.49	-14.04	-8.48	-29.01	4.44	15.19
2009	-5.55	-19.00	-8.34	-23.51	11.09	31.27
2010	-6.97	-19.66	-9.39	-24.44	11.20	29.14
2011	-5.30	-13.78	-10.92	-27.24	12.93	32.26
2012	-9.35	-23.32	-11.37	-25.72	12.37	27.97
2013	-11.29	-25.52	-12.01	-25.62	12.26	26.16
2014	-12.24	-26.12	-12.66	-26.22	13.41	27.77
2015	-8.26	-17.09	-9.74	-19.48	14.02	28.05
2016	-10.22	-20.44	-11.01	-21.48	14.99	29.25
2017	-11.54	-22.73	-13.24	-24.79	16.74	31.36
2018	-11.73	-21.97	-9.21	-16.27	16.41	28.97

Table 4.2:Current account and trade balance deficits and the cost of servicing the external debt are the three principal financial sources of the drain on the Lebanese economy. (Source: World Development Indicators database accessed on May 28, 2020)

	GDP pc	DB Database	SB Time	SB Cost	EC	Corruption	Credit	Informality	Mnf-%GDP	Hi Tech Exp	Rural Population	Female Labor	Education
Gini	-0.23	0.47	0.51	0.29	0.43	-0.18	-0.15	0.55	-0.35	0.06	-0.24	-0.31	-0.47
GDP pc		-0.43	-0.16	-0.31	-0.27	0.57	0.03	-0.20	0.23	0.19	-0.28	0.28	0.48
DB Database			0.51	0.66	0.54	-0.42	-0.55	0.47	-0.34	-0.30	-0.10	-0.48	-0.38
SB Time				0.19	0.07	-0.18	-0.23	0.26	-0.07	0.00	-0.06	0.05	-0.09
SB Cost					0.42	-0.32	-0.20	0.47	-0.06	-0.13	-0.03	-0.48	-0.39
EC						-0.28	-0.35	0.37	-0.31	-0.14	0.12	-0.32	-0.46
Corruption							0.24	-0.24	0.29	0.22	-0.03	0.23	0.39
Credit								-0.25	0.06	0.16	0.12	0.29	0.11
Informality									-0.20	-0.03	-0.37	-0.34	-0.21
Mnf-%GDP										0.28	0.10	0.09	0.23
Hi Tech Exp											-0.25	-0.04	0.21
Rural Population												0.07	-0.09
Female Labor													0.37

Figure 4.3: The correlation matrix of selected socio-economic indicators for the countries with higher than the average world GDP per capita (Source UNDP, 2017)

Description of the indicators used here:

Gini	Gini Coefficient.
GDP-pc	GDP per Capita, USD constant 2010 prices
DB Database	World Bank Doing Business Ranking - most to least favorable.
SB time	Average Number of days needed to start a business - World Bank DB sub-components.
SB cost	The cost needed to start a business as a percentage of income per capita - World Bank DB sub-components.
EC	Enforcement of Contracts, measuring time and cost for resolving commercial disputes through the first-instance court, and the quality of judicial processes.
Corruption	Corruption Perception Index, 2014 scores, (least to most favorable) - Transparency International20.
Credit	Getting Credit, World Bank distance to frontier score from 0 to 100 (least to most favorable) - World Bank DB sub-components.
Informality	Percent of Firms competing with unregistered firms
Mnf-%GDP	Manufacturing value-added as a percentage of GDP. As a

	percentage of total manufacturing exports.
Hi-Tech Exp	High Tech Exports as a percentage of total manufacturing exports.
Rural-pop	The rural population as a percent of the total population.
Fem	labor Female labor force participation as a percent of the total female population (15 years and above)
Education	Gross enrollment in secondary education, as a percentage of the population of official secondary education age.

In 2015 ------it reached a low of about 17%! Lebanon's trade balance has also been negative and has hovered around -20% of the GDP throughout this century. This has resulted in the mounting cost of servicing the country's external debt. The external debt has stayed at about 30% of the GDP over the past decade. Together, these three sources themselves amounted to a huge recurring drain on the national budget and worked out to a whopping US$ 37.35 billion in 2018, or two-thirds of the country's then GDP. The budget deficit and the external balance deficit are referred to as the twin towers of debt.

With negative numbers as large as these, the question is how the country has been surviving financially. As shown in Table 4.3, there have been three main sources to offset this deficit: remittances from the Lebanese workers overseas, Foreign Direct Investment (FDI), and the ODA (Overseas Developmental Assistance). As of October 2019, for instance, Lebanon's balance of trade was -574.2 million USD, the current account deficit was $240.6 million---- and external debt stood at $34.07 billion, according to the "Trading Economics" database. Compare these with the remittances of $836.8 million, FDI (Foreign Direct

Investment) of $231.8 million and gold reserves (largely frozen), and one can understand how significantly these personal remittances from the Lebanese workers in the neighboring countries have contributed to the Lebanese economy (Figure 4.4)

The remittances have contributed significantly to the country's economic survival (Kratou and Gazdar, 2015; Awdeh, 2018). But, though sizeable, these remittances of $4-5 billion per year or 12-13% of the Lebanese GDP, are still barely sufficient to meet Lebanon's external balance on goods and services. They can hardly dent the country's very substantial current account deficit and debt servicing costs. True, as shown in Table 4.3, two other funding sources also exist. They are the net FDI (Foreign Direct Investment) inflow and the net ODA (Overseas Development Assistance). But they are far too feeble when compared to the remittance inflows, and the size of the deficits.

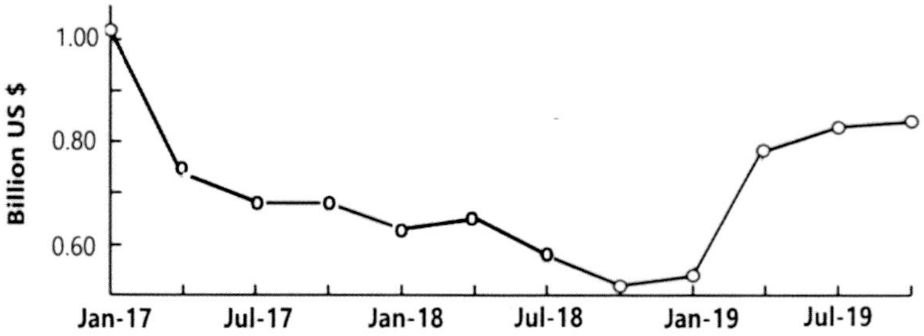

Figure 4.4: Quarterly remittances from the expatriate Lebanese workers (Source: https://tradingeconomics.com/lebanon/remittances accessed on June 17, 2020)

	Remittance Inflow		Net FDI Inflow		Net ODA	
	(bill US $)	(% of GDP)	(bill US $)	(% of GDP)	(bill US $)	(% of GDP)
2000	–	–	0.86	4.96	0.20	1.18
2001	–	–	1.45	8.22	0.20	1.11
2002	2.52	13.29	1.34	6.98	0.20	1.07
2003	4.08	23.62	2.25	11.20	0.58	2.88
2004	4.23	26.44	1.07	5.07	0.27	1.27
2005	4.01	22.91	1.91	8.88	0.23	1.10
2006	3.45	23.59	1.80	8.16	0.82	3.73
2007	2.96	23.19	2.53	10.16	0.98	3.92
2008	4.37	24.57	3.35	11.45	1.07	3.69
2009	5.75	21.30	3.68	10.37	0.58	1.66
2010	4.39	18.00	3.79	9.87	0.45	1.18
2011	4.38	17.16	2.20	5.49	0.48	1.20
2012	4.70	15.08	2.08	4.70	0.71	1.61
2013	4.95	16.15	0.68	1.46	0.62	1.32
2014	4.29	14.89	1.62	3.36	0.82	1.71
2015	3.68	14.97	1.50	3.00	0.97	1.94
2016	4.17	14.84	1.56	3.05	1.13	2.22
2017	4.45	13.25	1.20	2.25	1.30	2.45
2018	4.84	12.25	1.38	2.44	1.42	2.51

Table 4.3:The three principal financial sources of help to the Lebanese economy have been cash remittances from expatriate Lebanese workers, FDI inflow, and ODA. (Source: World Development Indicators database accessed on May 28, 2020)

These remittances started to dwindle since 2011 because the global financial crisis and job losses had limited the ability of the senders to make such transfers. A rise was recently observed, however. Significant numbers of these Lebanese expatriates live and work in the Arabian Gulf region and the continuing crisis there has made, on occasion, their employment situation unstable.

Interestingly, Lebanon is a heavily debt-ridden country but nowhere close to the world's highest national debt. That honor goes to Japan, with a total national debt of 9.09 trillion USD, and even the US national debt of 9.23 trillion

USD is way behind that of Japan. But Lebanon, with a total national external debt of $79.34 billion in 2018 or 149.7% of its GDP ranks amongst the top ten countries in terms of the debt to GDP ratio. The resulting external debt service thus claimed an equivalent of almost 30% of the country's GDP that year.

The origins of Lebanon's current financial quagmire can be traced back to several factors. Central to them has been the Central Bank's (BDL: Banque du Liban) monetary policy, particularly after the 2008 Great Recession worldwide. Since LBP (Lebanese Pound) was pegged to the US Dollar, BDL hiked its interest rates to attract more US Dollar deposits to help maintain the Lebanese pound's 22-year-old peg to the US dollar.

This rate hike was also expected to attract more depositors to fund the government's spiraling debt problem and to pay for Lebanon's enormous import bill. This was happening during the 2008 Recession when interest rates were declining in the world in order to stimulate economic growth. Eight years after that recession, the 10-year US Treasury constant maturity rate had dropped to 1.37%per year on July 8, 2016, See (https://fred.stlouisfed.org/series/DGS10).

At that time, BDL's deposit interest rate was 5.93% per year. That would have made perfect sense if the annual growth rate of Lebanon's GDP (Gross Domestic Product) was higher or the BDL was earning higher returns elsewhere. The GDP annual growth rate for Lebanon has averaged 6.68% for the entire 2000-2017 period, however, but was only 2% per year in 2016. It later turned negative.

The irony is that all these efforts were focused on attracting net FDI inflow of 10.2-11.5% of GDP during 2007-2009, which slowed down markedly to 1.5-3.4% of GDP during 2013-2018, even though BDL's USD reference lending rates rose from about 7% in 2018 to 9.7% by mid-2019. Foreign remittances from the Lebanese expatriate workers stood at 21.3-23.2% of the GDP during 2007-2009 ------and only at 12.3-16.2% of the GDP during 2013-2018. Also, these remittances came into Lebanon for local expenditures, whereas FDI proved to be more speculative than a stable long term investment.

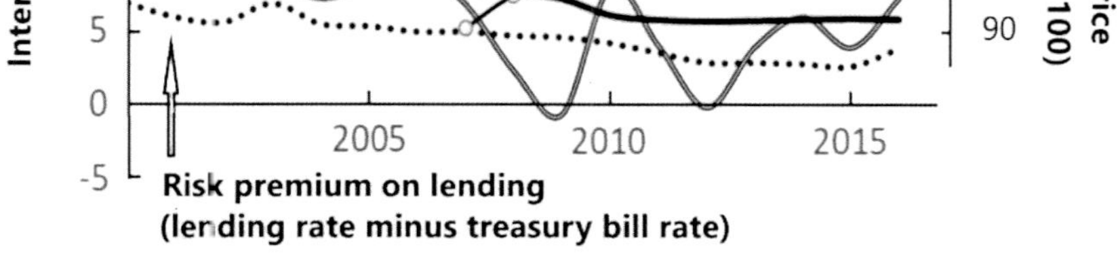

Figure 4.5: Lebanese central bank's interest rate history (Source: https://databank.worldbank.org/ accessed on June 19, 2020)

It can be said, therefore, that the peg of LBP to USD permitted Lebanese consumers to transact in their local currency and the US Dollars interchangeably, depositing their earnings in LBP one day and using that to import in

USD the next day, taking for granted the official exchange rate of 1507.5 LBP per USD irrespective of how much the country was importing in a given year and how much the country's foreign-exchange earnings (FDI and remittances) rose or fell in a given year. The false sense of security about the continuity of this peg increased conspicuous and luxury consumption and plans to encourage private investment in local manufacturing and agriculture to use these resources were lacking. This only encouraged wasteful consumption. For instance, the common man felt very comfortable driving luxury cars and over-sized imported SUVs, importing furniture, and booking personal travel loans to keep up with the Joneses, so to speak, often with no collateral other than their own basic salaries. This situation was not sustainable in a country with no steady inflow of foreign currency through exports of manufactured goods or explored resources like oil, or other high intellectual capital exports.

Economic Costs of Political corruption

Now, as for the issues of political corruption and administrative ineptitude, much of which is discussed in the rest of the book, a look at their socio-economic implications will be appropriate here.

Note that sectarianism has long been an important constraint in Lebanese politics, ever since the French mandate ended in 1943. This has been the crucial contributor to rampant corruption so prevalent in Lebanese society. High ranking government officials, because of their political and religious affiliations, felt immune from judicial prosecution and critical public scrutiny and had a free hand to forge self-serving contracts, inflate expenses, even charge personal expenses to ministerial accounts, and hire relatives as consultants.

They committed nepotism and smuggled on a grand scale, smuggling merchandise through seaports and other ports of entry, so depriving the government of tax revenue, just to name a few corrupt practices. It may now prove challenging to stop the current devaluation of the LBP vs. the US Dollar. However, it might still be conceivable for the LBP to hold steady the current black market level of the exchange rate in order to avert the ensuing severe political and socio-economic repercussions. This is reflected in Lebanon's rising "Economic Misery Index" shown in Figure 4.6[1] (Here we have used Steve Hanke's[2] modified version of the Barro Index as the sum of interest, inflation, and unemployment rates, less the year- on- year GDP growth). With March and April 2020 annualized inflation rates at 7.46% and 46.55% respectively, this index is alarmingly high.

Inflation and unemployment are the two issues that require swift action on the part of the government that may still be able to rein them in and restore public confidence in the local

---

1 As initially conceived by Arthur Okun, this index was the sum of inflation and unemployment rates, but Barro (1996) amended it by adding the Treasury bond yield and GDP growth rate.

2 Steve Hanke: https://www.cato.org/publications/commentary/misery-index-reality-check

economy. In order to accomplish this, a bundle of reforms needs to be quickly legislated, along with reforming public governance. The latter essentially involves ensuring the accountability of high ranking officials, through the judiciary, for their corrupt practices. The main challenge here is that too many public officials are involved in corruption. It will take political determination and a true sovereign central government to implement them. While the prevailing balance of power in the current government does not seem conducive for actions such as these, there is no reason why extensive use of information technology cannot facilitate achieving these objectives.

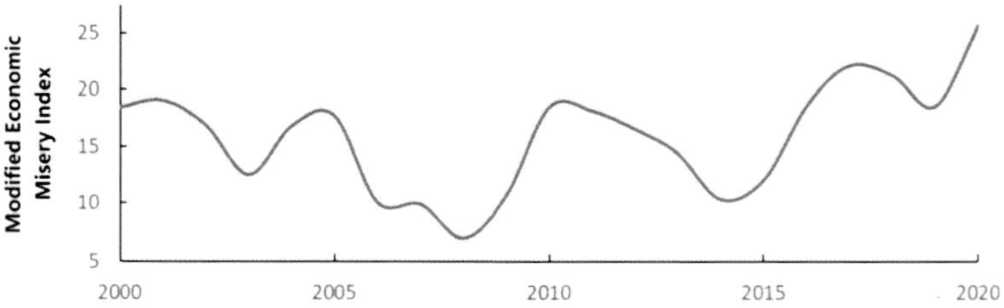

Figure 4.6: Lebanon's "Modified Economic Misery Index"– the sum of inflation, interest, and unemployment rates less the GDP growth rate. This index has been constructed here by interpolated the averages of the components where the original data were unavailable (Source data for 2000-2018 from https://databank.worldbank.org/ and for 2019-2020 from https://www.tradingeconomics.com/lebanon, both accessed on June 19, 2020)

The austerity measures in the recently proclaimed economic plan 2020 are likely to increase poverty and unemployment. As the political structure does not promote a culture of efficiently managing and operating public services, like utilities and public health, such plans will not be effective, no matter how generous foreign assistance is. It does not seem that radical solutions will be feasible without the formation of a government comprising political figures that enjoy independence, competence, national and moral stature, and the necessary courage and dedication to enacting the required reforms. Only then can these reforms possibly reclaim the trust of the citizens, investors, and the international community in Lebanon and its system of government.

Role of BDL in the Crisis

Banking and tourism are the most important sectors of Lebanon's service-oriented economy that were set back by several events: the Israeli invasion, the civil wars, and the massive inflow of refugees from the Syrian turmoil have forced the government to pledge vast resources towards constant reconstruction efforts. This, too, has added to a high level of public debt.

Lebanon, therefore, depends heavily on foreign aid in order to undergo reforms and strengthen the economy. Despite being a relatively free economy, foreign direct investments are hampered by bureaucracy, corruption, expensive utilities, and high taxes. All is reflected in the risk premium on Lebanon's debt carries. Figure 4.7 shows that the Lebanese interest rates have been consistently 5% points above the US Treasuries.

Table 4.4 shows recent credit ratings for Lebanon by the three major credit agencies, and these ratings are low enough to justify this high-risk premium.

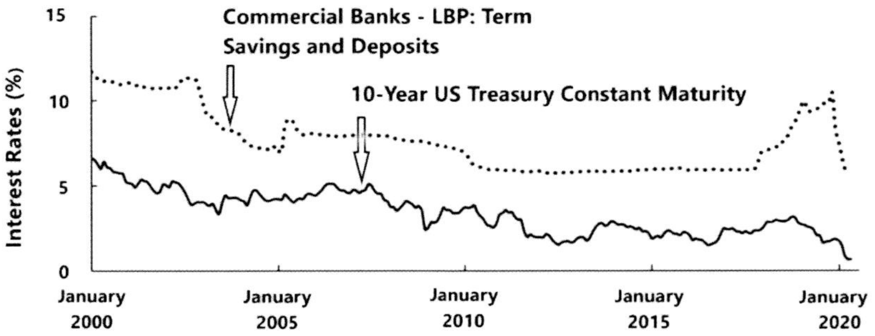

Figure 4.7: A comparison of Lebanese and US interest rates. The US data are for 10-year constant maturity US Treasuries, and the Lebanese data are for Commercial Banks – LBP for Term Savings and Deposits. Data sources are as follows: https://fred.stlouis

Fitch			S&P			Moody's		
Rating	Outlook	Date	Rating	Outlook	Date	Rating	Outlook	Date
RD	n/a	3/18/20	SD	n/a	3/11/20	Ca	stable	2/21/20
C	n/a	3/9/20	CC	negative	2/21/20	Caa2	under review	11/5/19
CC	n/a	12/12/19	CCC	negative	11/16/19	Caa1	under review	10/1/19

Table 4.4: Some recent credit ratings for the Lebanese government debts

The Lebanese money supply situation has deteriorated over the past one year, and, as Table 4.5 shows, volume losses in the currency deposits (LBP as also foreign) and the total money held by the non-banking system have been partially offset by substantial gains in M1, the currency in circulation. This apparently reflects a loss of faith in the banking system and hardly bodes well for BDL.

(in trillion LBP)	M1	M2	M3	M4
11 June 2020	25.51	58.42	194.88	206.39
11 June 2019	10.81	74.15	210.37	221.53
1 Year change	135.95%	-21.22%	-7.37%	-6.83%

Notes: M1: Currency in circulation
M2: Other deposits in LBP
M3: Deposits in foreign exchange
M4: TMs held by non-banking system including accrued interests

Table 4.5:Lebanon's current weekly money supply situation.

BDL is not to be faulted entirely for the country's current financial woes. The problem has been mainly ------the government's poor fiscal policies. ----------But problems arise when that monetary policy seeks to facilitate the government's wrong-headed fiscal measures?

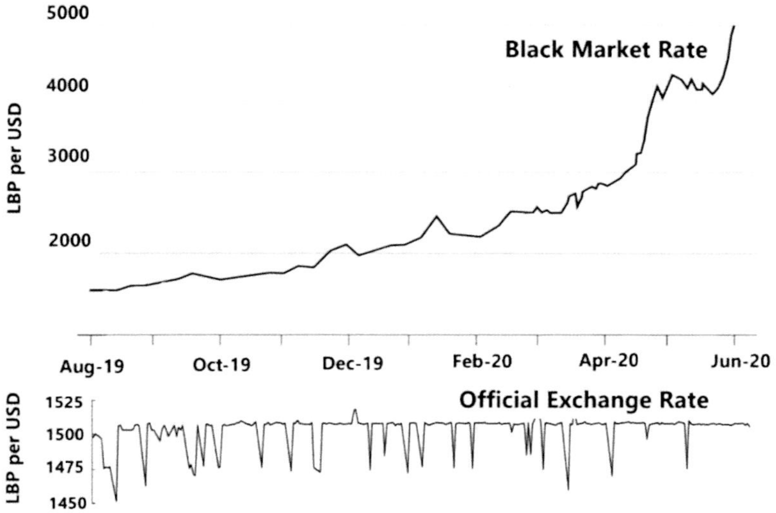

Figure 4.8: Lebanon's currency took a major tumble this year. The graph below shows that the official exchange rate continues to be about 1500 Lebanese pounds per UD dollar (shown in the bottom panel), whereas its value in the street, or the black market rate, is barely one-third as much (top panel). The solid line shows the black market rate, and is drawn here by combining the graphs from these two sources:

https://www.bloomberg.com/news/features/2020-03-11/lebanon-s-long-road-to-bond-payment-freeze-financial-crisis accessed on June 20, 2020, and https://finance.yahoo.com/quote/LBP%3DX/history?p=LBP%3DX accessed on June 25, 2020

Three interconnected but distinctly different factors that comprise the BDL's judgmental errors in this context immediately come to mind:

(a) Paying unsustainably high-interest rates to attract USD deposits.

(b) Financial engineering to support governmental borrowing.

(c) The obsession with the acquisition of foreign currency to maintain LBP's peg to the USD.

Lebanon became the banking capital for its neighborhood by pegging the LBP to the US Dollar, sustaining that peg for almost two decades, and paying high-interest rates to attract the deposits was simply not sustainable. It makes perfect sense, of course, to borrow money to meet one's expenses, be it for investment purposes or any other reason, provided that real possibilities exist to repay the loan in terms of the agreement. But it certainly made no sense to pay increasingly higher than usual interest rates just to attract the capital inflows that this low-exporting country needed, while part of the world was operating at negative interest rates.

Lebanon's annual inflation rate increased to 46.55 percent in April of 2020, the highest it has been since the series began in December of 2008, from 17.46 percent in the previous month, as the country faces its worst economic crisis in decades due to the collapsing LIRA. Prices rose faster mostly for food & non-alcoholic beverages (150.30% vs. 38.19% in March); transport (27.72% vs. 27.43%); alcoholic beverages & tobacco (167.42% vs. 45.90%) and clothing & footwear (135.09% vs. 33.93%). Meanwhile, housing & utility prices fell (-1.12% vs. 1.86%). On a monthly basis, consumer prices jumped 25.36 percent. This is all reflected in the black market exchange rate (figure 4.8).

These increases wiped out all advantages stemming from the interest rate differential between the US Treasury rate and the Lebanese commercial bank rate on dollar deposits in Lebanon. Add to this the sudden drop in the value of the Lebanese currency and the sudden illiquidity of bank deposits, especially those denominated in dollars, and the arbitrage across markets became unprofitable.

Figure 4.9 shows the history of the past three decades of Lebanon's FDI inflow from the three most important Arab sources: Saudi Arabia, Iraq, and Egypt. Notice the ebbs and tides of these inflows. Notice the association of 1997 and 2004 peaks of Saudi inflow with the late Prime Minister Rafik Hariri's tenures and of the 2007 dip with the crisis after his assassination. His son Prime Minister Saad Hariri's tenure also coincided with peaks in Arab investment inflows. Also noticeably discernible here are the effects of the War on Terror (2001 to the present), Arab Spring (2010 to the present), and the 2014 oil price crash.

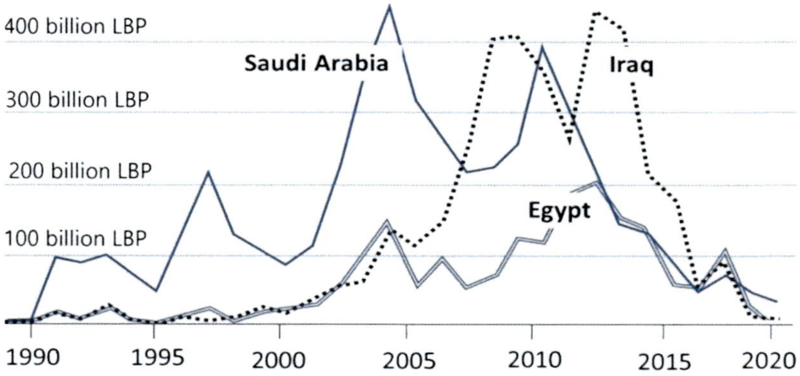

Figure 4.9: Much of Lebanon's FDI (Foreign Direct Investment) has historically come from her Arab neighbors and wealthy emigrants and has had ups and downs, reflecting the local political turns of events. (Source: https://english.alarabiya.net/en/features/2020/04/16/Lebanon-from-golden-age-to-economic-crisis-new-data-shows-rise-and-fall-Report.html)

The continuing, tumultuous record of the Arab world (Figure 4.9) and the turbulence of its own history, should not surprise anyone that FDI inflows from her immediate neighbors could hardly remain steady. To Holtmeier (2020), this made Lebanon "a refuge more than a magnet" for the foreign capital inflows.

Clearly, "relying on overseas dollars was a dangerous policy," as Larsen (2020) has pointed out. The central bank paid high-interest rates to attract foreign funds into the country, and yet the unsteady inflow of these foreign dollars could hardly cover the interest and capital payments. Actually, the central bank's financial engineering was what enabled the banks to pay exorbitant interest rates to big depositors out of the interest earned from their lending-- to the state. This resembles "a giant Ponzi scheme" in the words of Mounzer (2019) in a New York Times Op-Ed piece.

This second mistake by the central bank, the so-called

effective Ponzi scheme, resulted mainly from the efforts to solve the problem of unsteady and insufficient flow of foreign funds. But, promising such exorbitant interests to attract those dollar deposits to support the peg could have perhaps worked, if at all, either in a rising interest rate environment outside Lebanon (where BDL could have invested the flows) or where the funds thus attracted could have been used for productive and higher-yielding investments.

The bank's third mistake was an excessive obsession with the sanctity of its currency. $30 billion gushed into Lebanon in the aftermath of the 2008-2009 global financial crisis, due mainly to the high-interest rates at a time when the easing of money supply in advanced economies had produced near-zero interest rates. Maintaining foreign reserves became the be-all-and-end-all of all policies for the central bank (Hassan and Panizza, 2019). This resulted in having to pay "ever higher interests to attract dollar funds, even though these funds were not generating sufficient returns to repay the interest and capital," as these authors pointed out.

Lebanon's Unsustainable Fiscal Mess

Lebanon is currently facing limited options out of this quagmire. Clearly, the roots of this problem lie in four main drains on the economy — budget balance (or the lack thereof), total government debt-domestic and foreign debt, and the structural BOP problems. Abadi (2019) has examined one aspect of this problem, ascertaining if they are non-stationary, by conducting the Augmented Dickey-Fuller and the Phillips-Perron tests on 20 years long time series for these four datasets. He found that all the four series are only going to grow with time, ad infinitum, unless and until the current fiscal, monetary, and exchange rate policies change!

Two CFR (Council on Foreign Relations) blogposts, one by Setser (2020) and other by Asmar (2020), -----point to this uncertainty about the future of Lebanon's economy. For instance, Setser (2020) finds "good reason to think that Lebanon will not be able to defy financial gravity for much longer" as the "foreign currency deposit inflows that funded Lebanon's current account have dried up." Likewise, -----Asmar (2020), the only solution for Lebanon "is to commit to restructuring—irrespective of the pain it causes to the general public and to many stakeholders, particularly overindulged politicians—as a precondition for receiving the external funding it so desperately needs to stabilize the economy."

As for the IMF, the likely bailout agency that is still discussing a possible plan with the Lebanese authorities, the most recent statement is that "the size of the potential losses is quite large and the authorities are still discussing among themselves the choice of feasible options in terms of public debt sustainability and financial sector restructuring"[3] (IMF, 2020). On the question of the size of the likely bailout package, all that the IMF says is that discussions are focused on policies and reforms to restore macro stability and sustainable growth. Some argue that Lebanon's IMF rescue plan "fails to set reform roadmap." In contrast, others argue[4] that the "IMF bailout is no miracle solution for Lebanon" because there "is no reason to believe that those same people who have wrought despair upon their nation will be the ones to save it.' We could perhaps add here that most of the required fiscal and monetary measures will automatically fall in place once Lebanon decides to actually---------- dollarize its economy. This is our theme in the chapter to follow.

---

3 Transcript of June 18, 2020 IMF Press Briefing: https://www.imf.org/en/News/Articles/2020/06/19/tr061820-transcript-of-imf-press-briefing accessed on June 26, 2020.

4 https://www.thenational.ae/opinion/editorial/imf-bailout-is-no-miracle-solution-for-lebanon-1.1028921

Chapter 5
The Solution

A Quick Review of Economic Events

Lebanon has gone through substantial transformations since the end of the civil war in 1990. Many were the results of politics and wars such as Israel's Operation Grapes of Wrath in April 1996. The effects of such a war and the subsequent developments in Syria starting in 2011 had a major and speedy impact, as seen in Lebanon's GDP growth and capital flows. GDP growth during the period 2011-2018 averaged 1.7%, and for 2017 only 1.5%. It turned to a negative in 2019-2020. The 1990s saw substantial economic growth, with per capita GDP rising at about 7% annually, "inflation falling to 5%, and foreign exchange reserves rising to $6 billion" was suddenly in the rearview mirror. The Lebanese pound held steady at the official rate of LL1500/US dollar, as this was the consuming interest and preoccupation of the Central Bank (BDL).

The trigger for growth in the 1990s with GDP growth at 8% in 1994 and 7% in 1995 was a massive reconstruction program of $20 billion starting in 1993. Some slowdown in the reconstruction programs was experienced in the late 1990s as GDP growth slowed to 1% by 1999.

The banking sector during that period was also doing well, reflecting, once again, Lebanon's role as a "banking center" in the Middle East. By 2006 bank assets had reached $ 75 billion, and the small stock market was booming with the total capitalization of $10.9 billion (mostly from shares in Solidere and of key commercial banks).

The international financial crisis of 2007-2010 caused havoc in the world financial markets. However, the Lebanese economy was prospering again with GDP growth of 8.5% in 2008, 7 % in 2009, and 8.8% in 2010.

During all these periods, the national debt continued to rise. Lebanon became one of the most indebted countries in the world. That "distinction" never disappeared. The debt reached $90 billion in 2019 or about 190 percent of GDP. That sum incidentally did not include money owed by the government to the Social Security Fund, to hospitals, and private contractors. Even though Lebanon had a healthy primary balance in the budget on occasions, it was unable to generate enough funds to pay even the interest on the debt. Debt servicing plus interest thereupon amounted to one half of the government income. The rest went to public wages and corruption. Infrastructure projects are damned!

Professor Jad Chaaban of the American University of Beirut wrote in a Facebook post that the debt crisis "is the creation of a failed and criminal political class that lied and robbed for more than 30 years".

The results were predictable: Interest on the debt was capitalized in all future borrowings. This continued until 2020 when a new government declared it would default on its international debt:

"On Mar 9 Lebanon did not repay a $1.2bn Eurobond, the first sovereign default in the country's history. Even during the darkest days of its civil war in the 1980s, the state met its obligations," declared the Prime Minister added that "We will discontinue payment on all outstanding dollar-denominated Eurobonds." We note that 63% of public debt is Lira denominated.

At the end of January 2020, the Lebanese Central Bank (BDL) had $37 billion in gross foreign-currency reserves, but $52.5bn in liabilities mostly owed to local banks. These banks had 55% of their assets tied up at BDL. Some put that percentage as high as 66% (they are at 40% in other countries). Banks had every incentive to keep money with the central bank as the returns were lucrative and substantially higher than those on the public debt.

An 18% loss on these assets would leave commercial banks insolvent and require "a recapitalization worth at least 25% of GDP."

And the earth shook! Insecurity was everywhere amidst the Coronavirus. Debt cancellation and debt rollovers are not permissible. The man on the street understands that. Even his Falafel sandwich felt very expensive. Their demonstrations in the streets of Beirut went nowhere. They got rid of Hariri but kept the problems.

The Lebanese Lira began to collapse. It traded at as much as 200% below its official value. The problem continued, and the IMF is working out a solution in May of 2020. The Lebanese government is inept or unable to marshal enough resources to solve the problems without international assistance. The phantom of political intrigue and the contests between Saudi Arabia, Iran, and Israel for influence in Lebanon, and the extent of American interest and

France's in a solution dominated the public dialogue. Some saw Russians at the gate as well!

The run to safety became obvious. Large depositors with the banks withdrew $15 billion in 2019. Small depositors were restricted to only withdrawing $200 per week. The Oligarchs won again!

The effects were not symmetric across various communities. The poor became poorer, and organizations like Hizbollah were wary of supporting their social safety net. The voices of Christian leaders were muted.

With this background, we now look at a sensible, but a seemingly radical solution, which favors all the Lebanese.

The Role of the Dollar in the Lebanese Economy

Since 1990 Lebanon has had a parallel currency system using the local currency (the Lira) and the US dollar. The currencies were fully convertible almost anywhere in Lebanon at any time. All merchants accepted them freely at the official rate (1500LL/$), and deposits in banks can be initiated using either currency with full convertibility on demand. Dollar deposits could be transferred overseas and used for any domestic purpose.

Pegging the LL to the US dollar required that the Central Bank in charge of the peg to keep an ample supply of dollars. This setting was put in place to be equipped to intervene when needed. The Central Bank also needed to finance the critical imports of the government to include fuel costing $5 billion annually despite the untapped, massive gas and oil reserves Lebanon enjoys.

As of 2020, Lebanon was running a massive budget and balance of payments deficits (the twin towers of economic dislocation). The latter was $15 billion in 2019. Also, the economy was suffering from a severe recession: GDP growth in 2018 was -1.9%, -6.5 % in 2019, and expected to be -12% in 2020.

The introduction of the VAT tax and tax on interest income succeeded in trimming the budget deficits in 2003, 2004, 2005, and 2006. These reductions were consistent with the expectations of the Paris conferences. But the observers did not consider the effects of increased taxation on economic activity and especially on capital flows. They simply followed the French economic model and forgot about the wisdom of Ibn Khaldoun, as reflected in the Laffer curve.

The traditional model when Lebanon got into budgetary trouble relied on remittances. Some capital flows were for investment purposes or simply for arbitraging interest rate differentials between those offered by Lebanese banks and a domestic bank, typically in the United States. Also, dollars from Lebanese exports (meager in terms of imports) would flow to Lebanese banks. They (the banks), in turn, lend the money to the Central Bank (BDL), who will use the dollars to finance the government's international purchases of goods and services and to provide for market intervention to stabilize the LL. If all fails, the dollars will be borrowed by issuing Eurobonds.

The best and simplest business in Lebanon for the elite became banking. The most valuable asset to bank owners was the BANKING LICENSE itself. Banks were receiving dollar inflows paying interest on them at a higher rate than was offered in many western economies without any foreign exchange risk as the dollar peg was still holding.

The bankers then deposited them with the central bank often at outrageously high-interest rates while banks in Europe were receiving minuscule rates for their deposits with their central banks and often negative interest rates (see Khoury and Pal)

This stark picture is reflected in the fact that the international flows could not cover the twin deficits and not even the interest thereon. The current account was -14.7 billion in 2018, and -10.9 billion in 2019.

And now, with continued borrowing to cover these deficits, the Lebanese economy has gone full circle. The only alternative, many thought, was the international organizations: The World Bank and the IMF. Their involvement in Lebanon has burdened these organizations, and they will extract major concessions were they to continue with yet another rescue package.

The irony here is that the entrepreneurial and creative spirit of the Lebanese people to generate growth and progress were sidelined. Lebanon's true economic salvation must always rely on its enterprising people, good governance, stemming corruption, exploring Lebanon's natural resources such as oil and gas, paying a lot of attention to tourism by cleaning up the country starting with clean water and air in Beirut, and revamping the export sector. We discuss this further in the latter part of this chapter.

The Grand Solution

The preceding discussion makes clear that The Lebanese government cannot live within its means and that the Central Bank (BDL) has not been able to successfully deal with all the traditional functions of central banking-------. These functions are:

1- Issue the domestic currency

2- Keep the cash reserves (under the reserve requirements provision that maintains liquidity) of commercial banks and act as a lender of last resort

3- Control the money and capital markets by adjusting the money supply and, thus, interest rates.

4- Help the government finance its foreign purchases

5- Act as a custodian of the currency's exchange rate-ensuring the internal and external stability of the currency

6- Manage external debt.

BDL tried to manage the external debt through the years with mixed success. The out of control spending by the central government, the corruption, and the political intrigues and the unstable political structure left it invariably gasping for answers and reformulating strategies. All of these functions were assumed by BDL that would do anything to keep dollar deposits from the commercial banks flowing to its coffers so it can maintain the peg and make sure that the government can pay for its required imports especially oil, food, and flour.

Our Proposal

We are proposing the **full dollarization of the Lebanese economy** in order to stabilize the exchange rate permanently as a key foundation for economic growth. This is what this translates:

1- The adoption of the US dollar as a full replacement of the Lebanese Lira. The US dollar will become the medium of exchange, the unit of account, and the store of value for all Lebanese transactions within and outside Lebanon.

2- BDL will no longer serve as a lender of last resort

3- The Lebanese economy will be integrated in terms of monetary policy with the United States. All Lebanese financial institutions will have to improve their standards and levels of efficiency.

4- The credibility of the US financial system in the world will be Lebanon's

5- All foreign exchange rate risk relating to the Lebanese Lira will disappear. International investors coming to Lebanon will not worry about this risk. The remaining risk will be the volatility of the US dollar in the international markets. The world has effectively learned to cope with this volatility, and there are many instruments such as forward, futures, and options --- contracts to hedge it.

6- All bank accounts and loans will be denominated in dollars. Every person in Lebanon will transact in dollars

7- The risk premium Lebanon paid because of the uncertainty regarding the effectiveness of the peg will disappear. Lebanon will otherwise borrow at a lower rate internationally. Speculative attacks on the Lira would disappear much to the relief of the average Lebanese

8- Lebanon will forfeit monetary autonomy- It will no longer have unilateral control over its money supply. All dollars must be EARNED.

9- Transactions costs in the foreign exchange markets will be vastly eliminated

10- The Lebanese people will have a currency that can be used anywhere in the world. The Lebanese pound had no value outside Lebanon.

11- The saving rate in Lebanon is likely to rise as the concern about currency crises disappears

12- Substantial data on countries that have used dollarization in various forms (e.g., currency Boards) do exist. The case of Argentina (Orthodox Currency Board) and especially Panama (dollarization) are very instructive and should encourage the consideration of our proposal. Panama has many similarities with Lebanon as it is small, serves as a financial center, has a strong banking system, and its tourism is another major source of income. It also has a similar size population.

13- The risk of manipulating the currency system as such

exists, even in a currency peg or in a currency Board (a higher form of a peg), disappears, thus providing an overall gain.

14- Since dollarization will eradicate the issue of currency conversions, the calculation of HDI and relevant indexes to understand its impact on the Lebanese economy and the welfare of the Lebanese people, are further facilitated, e.g., one does not need to use the purchasing power parity to make realistic comparisons. Thus, this approach has statistical significance as well.

Many issues that academicians have been talking about, such as seignorage (the benefit that a country derives from issuing its own currency that can be used by the government to underwrite public expenditures) are sideshows for a small country. The cost of such was estimated at 0.3% of GDP for the larger countries. To really understand seignorage, look at the position the United States dollar occupies in the world economy. It allows the United States to print money to help control the effects of a Corona Virus, print money for the world to use, and run massive budget deficits without fearing an economic collapse, and to control the money supply of a large part of the world. No other country can do all these things.

Why in Lebanon

The Lebanese people are extremely familiar with the dollar. It is in their pockets, in their checking account and their investment and retirement plans. Once overseas, they use the dollar as they did in Lebanon. Its acceptability anywhere is typically unchallenged. They say that the dollar is king because it is.
For a long period, Lebanon has had a parallel currency system that worked without a major problem. Americans entering Lebanon, and there are a lot of them in the summers, can use their own currency to buy anything in Lebanon, to invest in Lebanon, and to hold a bank account in Lebanon. Lebanon has a laissez-faire system and enjoys considerable remittances from the United States and Latin America, especially.
US dollar deposits already account for about 70 percent of all deposits in Lebanon. Lebanese savers prefer dollars. The current crisis has taught them valuable lessons, as the pre-1990 collapse did.

Lebanon is already very dollarized

But the critical question remains: how does Lebanon get all the dollars it needs to make its economy function?
Only a **dramatic, comprehensive** approach executed in all its elements simultaneously will rescue the Lebanese economy. Here is what Lebanon must do to earn the needed US dollar to run a successful economy:

1- Reduce the reliance on traditional exports like olive oil and small manufacturing. Lebanon must rely going forward on exports with high intellectual capital. Its citizens have the training, education, and the will for it. Expanding agricultural exports is possible but limited by the size of the country. A shift into high-end agricultural exports such as Mango will indeed be wise. The Berytech Foundation in Beirut Lebanon recently launched the first Agri-food Innovation Cluster in Lebanon with the support of the government of the Netherlands" to serve as a platform for startups.
2- Lebanon, as was pointed out in an earlier chapter, has massive gas and considerable oil reserves. Their exploration and production must be the highest priority of the government. Schemes developed to freeze the government and the broader population from the benefits of oil and gas reserves must be trashed and their perpetrators exposed. At a minimum, Lebanon will save the $5 billion oil import bill. Lebanon will quickly become a net exporter of energy. This alone can cover the deficit in the current accounts.
The additional benefits are environmental in Character. As in many countries, even in China, car engines have been converted to run on natural gas. This will create an industry in Lebanon and will reduce pollution that suffocates the country, especially during the summer months, with a wide-ranging impact on tourism. The health benefits are also enormous.
3- Remittances. Lebanon has a huge number of immigrants

that have settled all over the world. Early in the 2000s, they accounted at one time for as high as 24% of GDP. There are 20 million Lebanese residing in almost every country in the world. Their financial success has, in some cases, been legendary. Carlos Slim of Mexico, the richest man in the world for four years, is just one notable Lebanese success story. Lebanon must encourage cooperation programs between the various communities and create programs for their children to visit Lebanon and learn about their cultures and history. Some of that is already taking place. It must be expanded as the old guard is disappearing.

Every dollar that enters Lebanon, it must be noted, has multiplicative effects on the economy. It can be calculated using the spending multiplier

$M = 1/(1\text{-}MPC)$

Where MPC is the marginal propensity to consume.

There are more factors that will affect the marginal propensity to consume, for example, level of taxation, availability of credit, consumer confidence, etc.

4- Foreign Direct investment in Lebanon. Lebanon needs to clean up its image as an inefficient country with a high level of corruption, and terrible infrastructure.

The authors know of numerous cases where deals were canceled because of the level of abuse and of the required size of the payoffs to officials and property owners. All basic services in Lebanon are expensive: electricity, water, telephones, cellular phone services, and fees of all types.

Improvements can be made at all levels to demonstrate to

the Lebanese immigrant population that they are indeed welcome and can thrive in Lebanon.

Once the corruption issue and the infrastructure issues are settled, Lebanon can become a hub for high valued exports. Its universities (and there are some good ones) produce a large number of engineers, mathematicians, technology experts, and physicists, etc. Every one of them loves to stay in Lebanon if assured of a good position commensurate with her education at a living salary. Currently, Lebanon is a huge exporter of brainpower. This must stop else the future of the country is doomed. The moment those students graduate, they scatter all over the Western and Arab Worlds, get deeply involved in their welcoming societies, educate their children, and increase the exports of their host country. Companies from the US and Europe tried to set up in Lebanon. Their tenure was short, and it sent discouraging signals. This must be reversed.

Tourism

Lebanon has traditionally gotten a good share of tourism. It has often been described as the Paris of The Middle East. Beautiful countryside and beaches, elegant shops, dynamic culture, high-end entertainment, and simply a fantastic cuisine covering most cultures have attracted millions of tourists.

However, its beaches are now polluted, the streets are not as clean, the air is suffocating during traffic congestions, and its political divisions are too transparent and project poorly on what is considered a historically superior culture.

With so many countries competing for tourist dollars, Lebanon is not winning. Some of the buildings in Lebanon are a reminder of a vicious civil war that unnerves every human being that reviews its history. Many of its landmarks are not well kept. Lebanon needs to clean up and realize its past success can be recreated and become a major source of foreign exchange.

Conclusion

This chapter clearly indicates that while Lebanon is indeed in trouble, the situation is not hopeless. Much can be done to reduce its deficits, stabilize its currency, and grow its economy.

We are to lay out a path for these outcomes. It is quite essential to signal a new age for Lebanon, which is a legal reform that will put some of the thieves of the national wealth behind bars. Every visitor to Lebanon is usually wary of getting scammed. Lebanon cannot afford such a reputation. It must stop. The transition into a dollarized economy will take a little time. The IMF should assist Lebanon on that short journey, especially with the conversion of the $8.8 billion Lebanese pounds now in circulation to dollars at an acceptable exchange rate. Also, the bankers in Lebanon must show they are willing to compromise and sacrifice for the national good. Their holdings of domestic debt in Lira should

be canceled. The bankers in Lebanon have already earned their principal investment many times over given the outrageous interest rates they received from BDL.

The Central Bank, BDL, must clean its balance sheet and insist on a fiscal reform that will once and for all force the government to live within its means. This starts with the reduction of the massive public payroll (including that of BDL itself), which is so politically charged. The rejuvenated private sector will be able to absorb the laid-off government employees. In addition to issues of refugees in Lebanon must be settled. Our proposal has proven to be helpful in many countries such as Ecuador, Montenegro, Panama, and even Zimbabwe as Dr. Steve Hanke has fully documented in his books and essays.

We trust that our proposal will be heeded, for the welfare of the Lebanese people depends on it.

References

Abadi, C. (2019) "Time is running out for Lebanon's unsustainable debt" Financial Times, Oct 20, 2019 (https://www.ft.com/content/e5d9cee1-b4fc-4b9c-95da-011b5db13b78 Accessed on June 25, 2020)

Asmar, A. (2020): "What's driving Lebanon's midpanademic protests?" Council on Foreign Relations blog post May 20, 2020 (https://www.cfr.org/in-brief/whats-driving-lebanons-midpandemic-protests, Accessed on June 26, 2020)

Awdeh, A. (2018), "The socio-economic effects of remittances in the labour-exporting MENA countries," International Journal of Emerging Markets, Vol. 13 No. 1, pp. 249-266. https://doi.org/10.1108/IJoEM-02-2017-0052

Barro, R.J. (1996): Getting It Right - Markets and Choices in a Free Society the MIT Press, 207 pp

Carnegie Middle East Center, Lebanon's Economic Crisis: A Ten Point Action Plan for Avoiding a Lost Decade, 2020

Cohen Benjamin, Dollarization: Pros and Cons, Working paper, UC Santa Barbara

Financial Times, many articles especially that of Chloe Cornish

Hanke Steve- we used several of his publications as references because: His international appointments also include state counselor to both the Republic of Lithuania in 1994-96 and the Republic of Montenegro in 1999-2003. He advised the presidents of Bulgaria (1997-2002), Venezuela (1995-96), and Indonesia (1998). He played an important role in establishing new currency regimes in Argentina, Estonia, Bulgaria, Bosnia-Herzegovina, Ecuador, Lithuania, and Montenegro. Hanke has also held senior appointments in the governments of many other countries, including Albania, Kazakhstan, the United Arab Emirates, and Yugoslavia.

Hamadi, Hassan, et al. "The effect of expatriate transfers on the Lebanese economy" International Journal of Business and Economics Perspectives, vol. 8, no. 1, 2013, p. 1+. *Gale Academic OneFile*, Accessed Jun 18 2020.

Hassan, F., and Panizza, U. (2019): "Understanding the Lebanese financial crisis." Financial Times, Dec 18, 2019 (https://ftalphaville.ft.com/2019/12/18/1576679115000/Understanding-the-Lebanese-financial-crisis/ Accessed on June 10, 2020).

Holtmeier, L. (2020): Lebanon from the golden age to economic crisis, new data shows rise and fall: Report; Al Arabiya English Thursday Apr 16 2020 (Source: https://english.alarabiya.net/en/features/2020/04/16/Lebanon-from-golden-age-to-economic-crisis-new-data-shows-rise-and-fall-Report.html extracted on June 25, 2020)

International Monetary Fund, Full Dollarization: The Pros and the Cons, 2000

Jakub Jaycay, Intra Bank, Lessons from Lebanon's First Banking Collapse, Koury S Institutional Competition as an Alternative Mechanism for Harmonization in Monetary and Banking Union. with Clas Wihlborg, Forum for EU Debate, Stockholm, 2014.

Khoury S,-Trust in the Euro and the Banking Union after Financial and Sovereign Crises, with Clas Wihlborg., book chapter by Palgrave Macmillan, 2017

Khoury S, Negative Interest Rates, with Poorna Pal, Journal of Risk and Financial Management, 2020

Kratou, H. and Gazdar, K. (2015), "Addressing the effect of workers' remittance on economic growth: evidence from MENA countries." International Journal of Social Economics, Vol. 43 No. 1, pp. 51-70. https://doi.org/10.1108/IJSE-08-2013-0189

Larsen, *N. (2020): "What is behind Lebanon's deepening financial crisis?" International Banker (Feb 10, 2020)* (https://internationalbanker.com/finance/what-is-behind-lebanons-deepening-financial-crisis/ extracted on June 25, 2020)

Mounzer, L. (2019): "The Great Lebanese Ponzi Scheme." The New York

Times, Dec 2, 2019 (https://www.nytimes.com/2019/12/02/opinion/lebanon-protests.html).

Moubayed and Zouein: Finding a Way Out of Lebanon's Crisis, 2020

Norton Augustus Richard, the Role of Hezbollah in Lebanese Domestic Politics, the International Spectator, Italian Journal of International Affairs, 2007

Saidi Nasser, Lebanon's Economy: Staring at the Abyss, 2020

Salloukh Bassel, Taif and the Lebanese State: The Political Economy of a very Sectarian Public Sector, Routledge, 2019

S&P: Lebanon's Banking Sector Shows' Similarities' to Greece Before, 2019

Setser, B.E. (2020): "Lebanon's Imminent Financial Crisis" Council on Foreign Relations Blog post Feb 18, 2020 (https://www.cfr.org/blog/lebanons-imminent-financial-crisis. Accessed on June 25, 2020)

Made in United States
North Haven, CT
05 November 2026

21757842R00064